THiNK

STUDENT'S BOOK 3

B1+

Herbert Puchta, Jeff Stranks & Peter Lewis-Jones

CAMBRIDGE
UNIVERSITY PRESS

CONTENTS

	FUNCTIONS & SPEAKING	GRAMMAR	VOCABULARY
Unit 1 **Life plans** p 12	Complaining Role play: Complaining to a family member Talking about the future	Present tenses (review) Future tenses (review)	Making changes Life plans **WordWise**: Phrases with *up*
Unit 2 **Hard times** p 20	Talking about the past	Narrative tenses (review) *would* and *used to*	Descriptive verbs Time periods
Review Units 1 & 2 pages 28–29			
Unit 3 **What's in a name?** p 30	Giving advice Expressing obligation Giving recommendations, warnings and prohibitions	*(don't) have to / ought to / should(n't) / must* *had better (not)* *can('t) / must(n't)*	Making and selling Expressions with *name*
Unit 4 **Dilemmas** p 38	Apologising and accepting apologies Talking about hypothetical situations Expressing wishes	First and second conditional (review) Time conjunctions *wish* and *if only* Third conditional (review)	Being honest Making a decision **WordWise**: *now*
Review Units 3 & 4 pages 46–47			
Unit 5 **What a story!** p 48	Telling a story	Relative pronouns Defining and non-defining relative clauses Relative clauses with *which*	Types of story Elements of a story
Unit 6 **How do they do it?** p 56	Talking about sequence Explaining how things are done	Present and past passive (review) *have something done* Future and present perfect passive (review)	Extreme adjectives and modifiers *make* and *do*
Review Units 5 & 6 pages 64–65			
Unit 7 **All the same?** p 66	Invitations Talking about permission Talking about habits	*make / let* and *be allowed to* *be / get used to*	Phrasal verbs (1) Personality **WordWise**: Phrases with *all*
Unit 8 **It's a crime** p 74	Giving and reacting to news Reporting what someone said, asked or requested	Reported speech (review) Reported questions, requests and imperatives	Crime Reporting verbs
Review Units 7 & 8 pages 82–83			
Unit 9 **What happened?** p 84	Making deductions	Modals of deduction (present) *should(n't) have* Modals of deduction (past)	Mysteries Expressions with *go*
Unit 10 **Money** p 92	Sympathising Talking about future events	Future continuous Future perfect	Money and value Jobs and work **WordWise**: *by*
Review Units 9 & 10 pages 100–101			
Unit 11 **Help!** p 102	Expressing purpose Emphasising	Verbs followed by gerund or infinitive *to / in order to / so as to* *so* and *such*	Danger and safety Adjectives with negative prefixes
Unit 12 **A first time for everything** p 110	Expressing regret Talking about fears	Phrasal verbs *I wish / If only* + past perfect	Phrasal verbs (2) Nervousness and fear
Review Units 11 & 12 pages 118–119			

PRONUNCIATION	THINK	SKILLS
Linking words with *up*	**Train to Think:** Reading between the lines **Self-esteem:** Life changes	**Reading** Article: I miss my bad habits Article: For a better life … Photostory: What's up with Mia? **Writing** An email about resolutions **Listening** A conversation about famous people who started their careers late
Initial consonant clusters with /s/	**Train to Think:** Following an idea through a paragraph **Values:** Animal rights	**Reading** Article: Events that shook the world Article: Family life in 17th-century Britain Culture: Where life is really hard **Writing** A magazine article about a historical event **Listening** A class presentation about animals being put on trial
Strong and weak forms: /ɒv/ and /əv/	**Train to Think:** Identifying the main topic of a paragraph **Self-esteem:** People and their names	**Reading** Article: Brand names Article: Crazy names Fiction: *Wild Country* by Margaret Johnson **Writing** A reply to a letter asking for advice **Listening** A conversation about techniques for remembering names
Consonant–vowel word linking	**Train to Think:** Thinking of consequences **Values:** Doing the right thing	**Reading** Quiz: What would YOU do? Article: The day Billy Ray's life changed forever Photostory: And the hole gets deeper! **Writing** A diary entry about a dilemma **Listening** A guessing game: Famous Wishes
The schwa /ə/ in word endings	**Train to Think:** Thinking about different writing styles **Self-esteem:** A better world	**Reading** Article: Everybody loves stories – but why? Article: Hollywood fairy tales Culture: Ireland – a nation of storytellers **Writing** A fairy tale **Listening** A conversation about a short story
The /ʒ/ phoneme	**Train to Think:** Understanding what's relevant **Self-esteem:** Life changes	**Reading** Article: The man who walks on air Blog: How Do They Do That? Fiction: *The Mind Map* by David Morrison **Writing** Explaining how things are done **Listening** A conversation about a new tattoo
Intonation – inviting, accepting and refusing invitations	**Train to Think:** Thinking outside the box **Values:** Stereotypes	**Reading** Film synopses: *Billy Elliot* and *Bend It Like Beckham* Article: My prisoner, my friend, my president and my father Photostory: The nerd **Writing** An article about stereotypes **Listening** A talk about a trip to Japan
Intonation – expressing surprise	**Train to Think:** Thinking about empathy **Values:** Respecting the law; Understanding that punishment will follow crime	**Reading** News reports: Thief feels sorry, Father angry victim of online con Article: Getting creative with crime Culture: Famous criminals **Writing** A report of a crime **Listening** An interview about restorative justice
Moving word stress	**Train to Think:** Fact or opinion? **Values:** Thinking carefully before you act	**Reading** Article: The truth is out there Article: Lost Fiction: *How I Met Myself* by David A. Hill **Writing** Explaining a mystery **Listening** A short story
Short and long vowel sounds: /ɪ/ – /iː/ and /ɒ/ – /əʊ/	**Train to Think:** Exaggeration **Self-esteem:** What's important for your future?	**Reading** Article: Bitcoins: here to stay? Web forum: Are they worth it? Photostory: Strapped for cash **Writing** My life in the future **Listening** A quiz show: *Show Me The Money!*
Strong and weak forms: /tuː/ and /tə/	**Train to Think:** Understanding cause and effect **Self-esteem:** Offering and accepting help	**Reading** News report: Local man's bravery rewarded Article: Emergency? What emergency? Culture: The Great Escape **Writing** A story about a rescue **Listening** The story of the farmer, the donkey and the well
Different pronunciations of *ea*	**Train to Think:** Logical conclusions **Values:** Breaking new ground	**Reading** Article: The first thing you remember Readers' letters: My first (and last) time Fiction: *Bullring Kid and Country Cowboy* by Louise Clover **Writing** A story about a bad decision **Listening** A presentation about the history of the Internet

WELCOME

A THAT'S ENTERTAINMENT!

let and *allow*

1 🔊 1.02 **Complete the conversation with the words. Then listen and check.**

~~looking~~ | allowed | makes | talent show | cross
songs | look | feel | sound | guitar | get | let

LISA Hey, Kim, what are you ⁰ *looking* at?

KIM My Science book. Can't you see I'm busy?

LISA I'm just asking. Sorry.

KIM No, I'm sorry. I don't ¹_____ great today.

LISA You don't ²_____ very happy. What's the matter?

KIM My dad ³_____ me so ⁴_____ .

LISA That doesn't ⁵_____ so good. Why?

KIM He says I'm not ⁶_____ to be in the band.

LISA What?! So he won't allow you to play in the ⁷_____ next week?

KIM No. He says no music until after my exams.

LISA But they don't finish for four weeks!

KIM I know. He wants me to study and forget about writing ⁸_____ . He won't even ⁹_____ me practise the ¹⁰_____ .

LISA But you need some time to relax.

KIM I know. I ¹¹_____ so angry when I think about it. It just isn't fair.

2 🔊 1.02 **Listen again. Answer the questions.**

1 Why is Kim angry?

2 How long is it until the exams finish?

3 What does Lisa think about the situation?

4 Who do you agree with: Kim or her dad? Why?

3 **SPEAKING** **What do your parents allow you to do during exam time? What don't they let you do? Make lists. Then compare with a partner.**

Music

Sort the words into two groups. Label the groups. Then think of four more items for each one.

drums | classical | jazz | violin
guitar | pop | piano | rap

Verbs of perception

1 **Complete the sentences from the conversation with the correct forms of (*not*) *look*. Then match them with the rules.**

1 You _____ very happy.

2 Hey, Kim, what _____ at?

> **RULE:** We use verbs of perception (*look, smell, feel, taste*) …
>
> in the **present continuous** to talk about **actions**. ☐
>
> in the **present simple** to talk about **states**. ☐

2 **Complete the mini-dialogues with the correct forms of the verbs.**

1 taste
   A What are you doing?
   B I _____ the soup … It _____ great.

2 smell
   A My socks _____ really bad!
   B Then why _____ you _____ them?

3 feel
   A Why _____ you _____ that jumper?
   B Because it's so soft. I like the way it _____ .

3 **Work in pairs. Kim tries to persuade her dad to let her play in the talent show. Write a conversation of eight lines. Then read it out.**

The big screen

1 **SPEAKING** Work in pairs. For each type of film, think of an example that you have both seen.

action | animated | comedy | drama | horror | romantic comedy | science fiction | thriller

2 Read the article. What types of films does it mention?

3 Read the article again and mark the sentences T (true), F (false) or DS (doesn't say).

1 Chris Columbus's films are popular with 13–18-year-olds. ☐

2 Columbus started making films when he was 30. ☐

3 His films aren't popular with older people. ☐

4 Lots of people in Hollywood want Columbus to make films. ☐

5 He's never won an Oscar. ☐

4 **SPEAKING** Work in pairs. Think of your favourite film director and discuss these questions.

1 What films has this director made?

2 What do you like about his/her films?

Present perfect tenses

Complete the sentences. Use the present perfect simple or continuous form of the verbs and circle the correct words.

1 They _____ (play) *for* / *since* 87 minutes and neither side has scored yet.

2 I *yet* / *still* _____ (not watch) the final, so please don't tell me which singer won.

3 _____ you _____ (see) last night's show *still* / *yet*? Brad Pitt and Lady Gaga were guests.

4 The children _____ (sit) in front of the TV watching *SpongeBob* *for* / *since* they got up.

5 It's the funniest programme on TV. I _____ (not miss) an episode *still* / *yet*.

6 The Prime Minister _____ (say) the same thing *for* / *since* weeks now. No one believes him.

Behind the camera

Chris Columbus

A 12-year-old who gets left behind when his family go on holiday, a teenage magician fighting to save his world and the troubled son of a Greek god living in modern-day America: these are just three of the characters brought to life on the big screen by director Chris Columbus. With films such as *Home Alone*, *Harry Potter and the Chamber of Secrets* and *Percy Jackson and the Sea of Monsters*, Columbus has certainly shown that he knows how to get teenagers into the cinema.

Columbus has been making films for more than 30 years and has become one of the most successful film directors of all time. Since he directed his first film, *Adventures in Babysitting*, in 1987, Columbus has been involved in some of the biggest films as both a director and a producer.

But Columbus doesn't only make action films for the teenage market. He's also made a number of successful films for adults. Comedies such as *Mrs Doubtfire*, dramas such as *The Help* and science fiction films such as *Bicentennial Man* have all helped make Columbus one of Hollywood's most popular film-makers.

TV programmes

1 Work in pairs. Look at the sentences in the previous exercise. Match them with the types of TV programme.

talent show | sitcom | cartoon | sports programme | the news | chat show

2 Choose a type of TV programme from the list below. Write a sentence about it using the present perfect simple and/or continuous. Don't include the type of programme in your sentence!

drama series | game show | reality show | soap (opera)

I've been watching it for weeks, but no one has won the million-dollar prize yet.

3 **SPEAKING** Read out your sentence. Can the rest of the class guess the type of TV programme?

B TIME TO ACT
Our endangered planet

1 SPEAKING Work in pairs. Describe the photos. What problems do they show?

 A

 B

 C

2 ◀)) 1.03 Listen to three conversations. Match them with the photos.

3 ◀)) 1.03 Listen again. In which conversation do you hear these words? Write the number.

a rubbish ☐   c litter ☐   e fumes ☐   g flooding ☐
b global warming ☐   d pollution ☐   f smog ☐

Question tags

1 Complete these sentences from the recording with the question tags.

are they? | aren't they? | does it?
did they? | is it? | isn't it?
weren't they? | doesn't it?

1 I guess they're just lazy, _____
2 But it only takes a few people to spoil everything, _____
3 Yes, it's all those fumes from the factory, _____
4 They didn't ask us if we wanted it here, _____
5 Even if they do, it doesn't make our lives any better, _____
6 Hundreds of homes were damaged _____
7 And the politicians aren't really doing anything to help, _____
8 It isn't the sort of thing you'd expect to see here, _____

2 Complete the sentences with question tags.

1 You haven't told Ron, _____?
2 You're going to do something about it, _____?
3 It sounds quite dangerous, _____?
4 It didn't work, _____?
5 It won't be easy, _____?
6 She wrote to her local politician, _____?

So do I / Neither do I

1 Look at the questions and complete the answers with *so* or *neither*.

1 A I don't really believe in all that.
   B _____ do I.

2 A I think we should do something.
   B _____ do I.

2 SPEAKING Complete the sentences so that they are true for you and read them out. Agree (or disagree!) with your partner's sentences.

1 I really like _____
2 I don't like _____
3 I believe _____
4 I don't believe _____

Accepting and refusing invitations

1 ◀)) 1.04 Put the sentences in order to make a conversation. Then listen and check.

1	SUE	Marco and I want to do something to help the flood victims.
	SUE	Yes – 20 km! <u>Want to join us?</u>
	SUE	<u>That's a shame.</u> But <u>you will</u> sponsor us, <u>won't you?</u>
	SUE	We're going to do a sponsored walk next Sunday.
	DEREK	<u>Of course I will.</u>
	DEREK	Are you going to walk a long way?
	DEREK	What are you going to do?
	DEREK	<u>I'd love to, but I can't.</u> I'm busy.

2 Work in pairs. Write a conversation using the <u>underlined</u> phrases from Exercise 1.

You and your friend are tired of all the rubbish in the street and have decided to do something about it. What are you going to do? Invite another friend to join you.

Party time

1 Work in pairs. Imagine you're organising a party. Make a list of important things to do.

2 Read the article. Does it mention the things on your list?

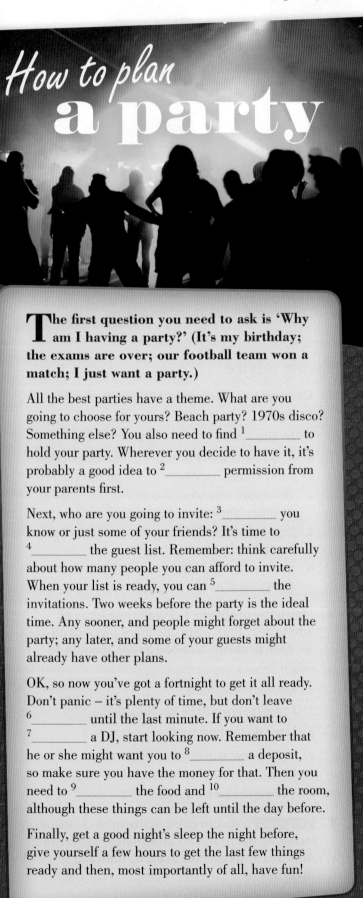

How to plan **a party**

The first question you need to ask is 'Why am I having a party?' (It's my birthday; the exams are over; our football team won a match; I just want a party.)

All the best parties have a theme. What are you going to choose for yours? Beach party? 1970s disco? Something else? You also need to find ¹_____ to hold your party. Wherever you decide to have it, it's probably a good idea to ²_____ permission from your parents first.

Next, who are you going to invite: ³_____ you know or just some of your friends? It's time to ⁴_____ the guest list. Remember: think carefully about how many people you can afford to invite. When your list is ready, you can ⁵_____ the invitations. Two weeks before the party is the ideal time. Any sooner, and people might forget about the party; any later, and some of your guests might already have other plans.

OK, so now you've got a fortnight to get it all ready. Don't panic – it's plenty of time, but don't leave ⁶_____ until the last minute. If you want to ⁷_____ a DJ, start looking now. Remember that he or she might want you to ⁸_____ a deposit, so make sure you have the money for that. Then you need to ⁹_____ the food and ¹⁰_____ the room, although these things can be left until the day before.

Finally, get a good night's sleep the night before, give yourself a few hours to get the last few things ready and then, most importantly of all, have fun!

3 **Read the article again and complete it with the missing words.**

get | send out | organise | pay
everyone | hire | decorate
somewhere | draw up | everything

Indefinite pronouns

1 🔊 1.05 **Complete the conversation with suitable indefinite pronouns (*everyone*, *somewhere*, *nothing*, etc.). Then listen and check.**

TOM   Have you got ¹_____ ready for the party?

JADE No, ²_____ is ready. We haven't found ³_____ to have it, for a start. We've looked ⁴_____ .

TOM   Have you invited ⁵_____ yet?

JADE Yes, we've invited 50 people and ⁶_____ is coming!

TOM   So you've got 50 people coming, but ⁷_____ for them to come to?

JADE That's right.

TOM   Well, we've got to do ⁸_____ . How about using my house?

JADE What about your parents?

TOM   They won't mind. They're going ⁹_____ for the weekend. I'll make sure ¹⁰_____ is clean and tidy when they get home.

2 **Read the next part of the story and continue the conversation. Write four more lines. Use at least one indefinite pronoun.**

It's the day after the party. Tom's mum and dad arrive home and open the door …

MUM   What's happened? Look at our house!

DAD   Tom! TOM!

TOM   Oh, hi, Mum. Hi, Dad. You're home early. Did you have a good time?

Arranging a party

SPEAKING Work in pairs to organise a party. Be creative! Think about:

- what it's for
- the theme
- who to invite
- where it will be
- food and drink
- music

C IN MY OPINION, …
Feeling under the weather

1 🔊 1.06 **Listen to the conversation. What's the matter with Gemma?**

2 Complete the conversation with the words.

appointment | should | operation
energy | better | get | physically | took

MUM You don't look well, Gemma. What's up?

GEMMA I'm just tired all the time, Mum. You know, I haven't got any ¹_____ .

MUM Are you sleeping OK?

GEMMA Not great, no. I often wake up in the night.

MUM Well, you know, Gemma, you ²_____ take more exercise. That would help.

GEMMA Really?

MUM Yes. I mean, if you ³_____ more exercise, you'd be more tired ⁴_____ and then you'd sleep better.

GEMMA You're joking, right? I run, I go swimming, I go for long walks. My problem isn't exercise.

MUM Yes, you're right, of course. Well, perhaps you'd ⁵_____ see a doctor. I can ring and make an ⁶_____ for you if you like.

GEMMA A doctor? I don't think so. I don't feel sick – just tired. I'm sure I'll ⁷_____ better soon.

MUM OK, well, we can talk about it later. I'm going out to see a friend of mine who had an ⁸_____ last week.

GEMMA OK, Mum. Hope your friend's all right. And don't worry about me. I'll be fine.

3 Match the verbs 1–6 with a–f to make phrases. Sometimes there's more than one possible combination.

1	feel	a	an appointment
2	get	b	an operation
3	have	c	exercise
4	make	d	a doctor
5	see	e	better
6	take	f	sick

4 Write down as many words related to health as you can think of. Then compare with a partner.

sick
nurse
hospital
…

Giving advice

1 Complete the sentences with *better*, *should* or *ought*.

1 It's late – you'd _____ go.
2 If you aren't well, you _____ to see a doctor.
3 Jane's in hospital. We _____ go and visit her.
4 The doctor is very busy, so you _____ make an appointment. Don't just turn up.
5 Your knee hurts? Well, you'd _____ not play football today, then.
6 If you want to get better, you _____ to rest as much as possible.

2 Match the problems 1–3 with the pieces of advice a–c. Then write one more piece of advice for each problem. Use *had better*, *should* and *ought to*.

1 My hand really hurts. ☐
2 I think I'm going to be late for school. ☐
3 I can't do this homework. ☐

a You'd better hurry.
b Perhaps you should phone a friend.
c You ought to see a doctor.

3 **SPEAKING** Work in pairs. Write mini-dialogues including the problems and advice in Exercise 2. Add two or three lines to each. Then act them out.

Why all these awards?

I'm really tired of awards ceremonies and prizes. Why do we have to compare things? Everywhere you look, there's something going on about who or what is 'the best' or 'the most comfortable' or 'the biggest', and so on. And sometimes the prize winners aren't the best anyway!

Here's an example: the Oscars in 2014. I saw the film *Gravity* and it was the most exciting film I'd ever seen. But did it win the Oscar for Best Film? No! They gave the award to *Twelve Years A Slave*! Can you believe it? It wasn't as good as *Gravity* at all.

OK, *Gravity* was the most successful film at the Oscars – it got seven awards – but I don't think that's enough. Sandra Bullock was fantastic as Dr Ryan. I think she's much better than Cate Blanchett, who won Best Actress. But the good thing is that *Gravity* won Best Visual Effects – I've never seen anything as fantastic. And was the music good? It was great! No other film had music as brilliant as that.

I said all these things to my friend Dave the day after the Oscars. I told him I thought the judges were the craziest people in the world. Dave asked me how many films I'd seen in 2013. I said, 'One – *Gravity*.' Dave says he doesn't know anyone as stupid as me.

Better or worse?

1 Read the blog entry. Mark the sentences T (true) or F (false).

1 The writer likes awards ceremonies. ☐

2 *Gravity* won Best Film at the 2014 Oscars. ☐

3 The writer thinks the visual effects in *Gravity* are the best he's ever seen. ☐

4 Dave thinks the writer is very intelligent. ☐

2 SPEAKING Work in pairs. Discuss these questions.

1 What other awards ceremonies do you know of?

2 Do you like awards ceremonies? Why (not)?

3 Do you think it's fair to compare different movies, actors, music, etc. and choose one as the best?

Comparisons

1 Complete the sentences with the correct form of the adjectives and adverbs. Add any other necessary words.

1 The weather tomorrow won't be _____ (cold) as today.

2 This is the _____ (good) pizza I've ever eaten.

3 Do you think this is _____ (difficult) than the other test?

4 This book's OK, but it isn't the _____ (interesting) one I've ever read.

5 She learns things _____ (easy) than I do.

6 I'm not very good at tennis, but I'm _____ (bad) as Janice!

7 Hurry up! Can't you walk _____ (quick) than that?

8 Do you speak as _____ (loud) your sister?

2 SPEAKING Work in pairs or small groups. Discuss these statements. Do you agree or disagree with them? Why?

1 The best things in life are free.

2 If something is more expensive, it's always better.

3 It's more important to work hard than to play hard.

4 Exercise isn't as important as good sleep.

3 Choose two things or people from one of these categories. Write a paragraph comparing them.

sports that you like | actors that you like
towns or cities that you know | school subjects
books that you have read

D HELP!
Reported speech

1 Read the story and answer the questions.

1 What had happened to the caller's computer screen?
2 What three things did Graham ask the caller to do?
3 Why couldn't the caller switch on the lights?
4 What did Graham finally say to the caller?
5 What happened to Graham in the end?

We asked readers to tell us about a time when they tried to help someone. Here's one from Graham Smith.

I used to work in IT for a big company, but I was fired because I got angry with a manager. Here's what happened.

I answered the phone one day and said, 'Hi. Can I help you?' A voice said, 'Hi. I'm a manager in the Sales Department and I've got an IT problem. I need your help.' 'What's the problem?' I asked, and he told me his computer screen had suddenly gone black.

¹_____ , I couldn't think why it had happened. I asked him to check that the screen was still connected. He said it was. ²_____ I asked him if he'd pressed any buttons by mistake. He said, 'No, the computer was installing a program when, suddenly, it went "pooff".'

³_____ a few seconds, I said, 'OK, please check that your computer is still plugged in at the wall. Sometimes it gets disconnected accidentally.' The manager asked me to wait a bit. Then he came back and said, 'I can't see behind my desk where the plug is. It's very dark.' So I told him to switch the light on. Do you know what he said? 'Oh, I can't put the light on because the electricity went off five minutes ago.'

I tried to keep quiet. ⁴_____ , I had to say something. I warned him never to phone me again, ever. He complained to my boss and I was fired. How fair is that, do you think?

2 Rewrite the sentences in reported speech.

0 'I need your help.'
He said that ___*he needed my help.*___

1 'What's the problem?'
I asked him _____

2 'I can't see here because it's very dark.'
He said that _____

3 'Please check that your computer is still plugged in.'
I asked him to _____

4 'I can't put the light on because the electricity went off five minutes ago.'
He said that _____

Sequencing words
Match these words with spaces 1–4 in the story.

a After ☐   c Finally ☐
b Then ☐   d At first ☐

Asking for and offering help

1 Put the words in order to make questions.

1 I / you / Can / help / ? ☐
2 help / something / you / me / Could / with / ? ☐
3 me / you / Can / a / lend / hand / ? ☐
4 you / Do / help / any / need / ? ☐
5 you / minutes / got / a / Have / few / ? ☐

2 Look at the sentences in Exercise 1 again. Mark them A (asking for help) or O (offering help).

3 SPEAKING Work in pairs. Choose a situation and write a conversation in which A asks B for help. Use expressions from Exercise 1. Then act it out.

- A has a problem with some homework.
- A isn't feeling well.
- A's computer isn't working.
- A wants to have a party, but doesn't know where to hold it.

IT problems

1 **SPEAKING** Work in pairs. What do the pictures show?

A ☐

B ☐

C ☐

2 **◀)) 1.07** Listen to three conversations. Match them with the pictures in Exercise 1.

3 **◀)) 1.07** Listen again. In which conversation do you hear these words? Write the number.

a	attachment	☐	e	install ☐
b	coverage	☐	f	online ☐
c	downloaded	☐	g	program ☐
d	file	☐	h	upload ☐

IT vocabulary

1 (Circle) the correct words.

1 *go / have* online
2 *post / file* a message
3 *install / key in* your password
4 *install / go* a program
5 *attach / activate* a file
6 *download / go* a file
7 *upload / key* a photo
8 *key / delete* a message
9 *open / install* an attachment
10 *post / buy* an app
11 *upload / activate* flight mode
12 *have / go* network coverage

2 Match the verbs with the nouns. Make as many combinations as you can.

a message | a photo | flight mode | a password
an attachment | a program | a file | an app

0	install	*install a program / an app*
1	attach	_____
2	download	_____
3	upload	_____
4	open	_____
5	post	_____
6	delete	_____
7	activate	_____
8	key in	_____

Passive tenses

1 Complete the sentences from the conversations with the verb forms.

is being repaired | was taken | is installed

1 The photo _____ on a safari trip.
2 Just click on it and the program _____ automatically.
3 The network _____ out here.

2 Rewrite the sentences in the passive.

0 Someone posted a message.
   A message was posted.
1 Someone is downloading a program.
   _____
2 Someone has installed a new program.
   _____
3 Someone has keyed in the password.
   _____
4 Someone is repairing the anti-virus software.
   _____
5 Someone deleted the message.
   _____

3 Describe one of these processes using the passive.
   • downloading an app to your mobile phone
   • uploading a photo to a social networking site
   • installing a program on your computer

11

READING

1 What are the people doing in the photos? Do you think these are good or bad habits? Why?

2 Tick (✓) the bad habits that you have. Then add two more of your own.

- ☐ not doing enough exercise
- ☐ leaving your homework until the last minute
- ☐ forgetting important dates
- ☐ texting when you shouldn't
- ☐ playing computer games when you should be studying
- ☐ getting up late for school

3 `SPEAKING` Work in pairs. What can you do to change some of these habits?

4 Read the article quickly. What two things is the writer trying to change about her life?

5 🔊 1.08 Read the article again and listen. Mark the sentences T (true) or F (false).

1 The writer has to finish the article by the following day. ☐

2 The writer is finding it easy to lead a healthier life. ☐

3 We use different parts of our brain depending on who we're thinking about. ☐

4 Our brains don't always let us make good choices for our future selves. ☐

5 It takes just under two months for our brains to feel happy with changes to our lifestyles. ☐

6 The writer has decided that she'll never be able to change her habits. ☐

I miss my bad habits

I don't believe it! It's 11 pm and I'm still sitting here writing this article for the school magazine! I've had two weeks to write it and my teacher wants it tomorrow. She's always complaining that I leave things to the last minute. Maybe she's right. A month ago, I made a resolution to be more efficient this year and to never leave things to the last minute. Well, I've failed. At the moment, I guess kids all over the country are thinking back to the resolutions they made at the beginning of the school year. Some of them have already given up for this year. Others are still doing well. Many, I suspect, like me, are struggling with them. I've also been trying to get fitter for four weeks now. I've started going to the gym, I've taken up karate lessons and I've changed my diet. I've even been going to bed earlier. But I'm not feeling any fitter, just a little unhappier. I miss my bad habits. Why is leading a better life so hard?

I've just read an article on a website and I've discovered that it isn't my fault! In fact, it isn't anyone's fault. It's our brains. They're programmed to make it difficult to break bad habits. There's nothing we can do. For example, you're sitting up late playing Minecraft. You know you've got an important test tomorrow, so why don't you just turn off the computer and go to bed? As I said, it's your brain's fault. Scientists have done experiments that show we use one part of our brain when we think about ourselves and another when we think about other people. However, when we think about ourselves in the future, we use the same part of the brain that we usually use to think about other people. In other words, the brain sees the 'future you' as a different person to your 'present you'. And that's why we don't always find it easy to make sensible decisions for ourselves in the future.

But that's not all. Scientists have also discovered that it takes around ten weeks to form a good habit. For example, it's going to take another six weeks before going to the gym stops being so difficult and becomes an automatic part of my life. That's because ten weeks is the amount of time the brain needs to change and accept new behavioural patterns as part of everyday life. The good news is that once you make it to ten weeks, everything becomes a lot easier. The bad news is that ten weeks is a really long time, so it's easy to give up on your good intentions sooner.

So there you are. Maybe we want to change our ways and become better people but our brains won't let us. Or is this just an excuse? Look – I've finished my article on time! Anything is possible!

■ TRAIN TO THiNK ■

Reading between the lines

Sometimes a writer doesn't tell us everything directly: we need to draw conclusions from the information the writer gives. We call this 'reading between the lines'.

6 **Answer the questions and give reasons for your answers.**

   0 Who is the writer? (paragraph 1)
      She's a schoolgirl — she's writing for the school magazine and mentions her teacher.

   1 Does the writer feel guilty that she hasn't finished the article? (paragraph 1)

   2 Does she enjoy exercise? (paragraph 1)

SPEAKING

Work in pairs. Discuss these questions.

1 What resolutions are you going to make for this school year?

2 What do you think is the secret of changing your life for the better?

   Careful planning.   *Do work first, play later.*

   Listen to your parents.

GRAMMAR
Present tenses (review)

1 **Match sentences 1–5 with the tenses a–d and then complete the rule with the names of the tenses.**

1 I'm still **sitting** here writing this article.
2 I've also **been trying** to get fitter for four weeks now.
3 I've **started** going to the gym.
4 I'm **not feeling** any fitter, just a little unhappier.
5 The brain **sees** the 'future you' as a different person to your 'present you'.

a present perfect continuous
b present simple
c present continuous (x2)
d present perfect

RULE:

1 We use the _____ to talk about facts and give opinions.
2 We use the _____ to talk about what's happening at or around the time of speaking.
3 We use the _____ to talk about past actions without saying when they happened.
4 We use the _____ to talk about actions that started in the past and are still happening.

LOOK! We can use the present continuous with *always* to complain about behaviour that we don't like and find annoying.
My dad's always telling me what to do.

2 **Complete the text with the correct present tense forms of the verbs. Sometimes more than one tense is possible.**

It's 2 am and I [1]_____ (lie) in bed. I [2]_____ (try) to get to sleep, but I can't. I [3]_____ (have) trouble sleeping for about a month now. I [4]_____ (try) different things to help me sleep, but nothing [5]_____ (work). My mind [6]_____ (not want) to stop. A lot [7]_____ (happen) in my life right now. It's exam time, so I [8]_____ (study) a lot. There's also the question of next year. I [9]_____ (think) about it for ages. Mum and Dad [10]_____ (want) me to go to university, but I'm just not sure what to do.

3 **SPEAKING** Work in pairs. Think about a problem you've been having and tell your partner.

I've been fighting a lot with my little brother recently. I've tried to ignore him, but it's impossible.

Workbook page 10

VOCABULARY
Making changes

1 **Match the phrases with the definitions.**

0 make a resolution — *f*
1 give something up — ☐
2 do well — ☐
3 struggle with something — ☐
4 take something up — ☐
5 break a bad habit — ☐
6 form a good habit — ☐
7 change your ways — ☐

a stop doing something
b find something difficult
c start a new hobby or interest
d stop doing something that isn't good for you
e start doing something that is good for you
f decide to make a positive change
g do things differently (usually for the better)
h be successful

2 **Complete the text with the missing verbs.**

Last year I [1]_____ loads of resolutions and decided to [2]_____ my ways. I tried to [3]_____ the habit of getting up late at weekends. For two months I got up at 8 am. But by 2 pm I felt sleepy, so I [4]_____ up sleeping in the afternoon. I also [5]_____ up wasting time online, but my parents bought me a laptop and that was the end of that. Then I stopped eating meat. I was [6]_____ well until Mum made roast beef. I just had to eat it. I tried to [7]_____ good habits as well: for example, I started piano lessons. But I [8]_____ with finding time to practise, so I stopped. This year I've only made one resolution: not to make any resolutions.

3 **SPEAKING** Work in pairs. Discuss these questions.

1 What subjects are you doing well in at school?
2 What subjects do you struggle with?
3 What was the last thing you gave up doing? Why?

Workbook page 12

LISTENING

J.K. Rowling

Sylvester Stallone

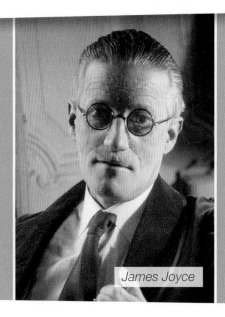
James Joyce

1 **SPEAKING** **Work in pairs. Discuss these questions.**

1 What do you know about these people?

2 Can you match the information with each person?

A _____ was a famous Irish writer.

B _____ wrote *Rocky*.

C _____ wrote the Harry Potter series.

2 ◀)) 1.09 **Listen and check.**

3 ◀)) 1.09 **Read the questions carefully. Listen again and make notes.**

1 What's Annie's problem?

2 What does Ben want to do with his life?

3 How was James Joyce earning a living when he was 30?

4 How are the examples of Joyce, Stallone and Rowling different to Annie's situation?

5 Why does Ben tell Annie not to worry?

4 **SPEAKING** **Work in pairs. Compare your answers to Exercise 3.**

GRAMMAR
Future tenses (review)

1 **Look at the sentences from the listening. Complete them with the correct future forms of the verbs. Then complete the rule with *present continuous*, *going to* and *will*.**

1 I _____ (meet) the careers advisor this afternoon.

2 I _____ (study) medicine at university.

3 I'm sure you _____ (do) well whatever you do.

> **RULE:**
> - To talk about future arrangements, we often use the [1]_____ .
> - To make predictions, we often use [2]_____ .
> - To talk about intentions, we often use [3]_____ .

2 Circle **the best tense.**

1 *We'll go / We're going* to the beach this Friday. Do you want to come?

2 I don't think *I'll finish / I'm finishing* this homework.

3 *I won't go / I'm not going* to university this year. I want to take a year off.

4 I've got an appointment with the dentist tomorrow. *I'm seeing / I'll see* her at 10 am.

5 Daisy's learning to fly. *She'll be / She's going to be* a pilot.

6 I'm not *eating / going to eat* chocolate. That's my resolution for next year.

7 Argentina *will win / are winning* the next World Cup. That's what I think.

8 *We're flying / We will fly* on Friday. I'm so excited.

3 **Write down:**

1 two arrangements you've got for this week.

2 two intentions you've got for this year.

3 two predictions for your life.

Workbook page 11 ➤

READING

1 SPEAKING Tick (✓) the statements you agree with. Then discuss them in pairs.

A good friend …

☐ always tells you what they're thinking.

☐ never criticises you.

☐ agrees with everything you say.

☐ always listens when you have a problem.

2 Read the article and match the titles with the paragraphs.

☐ No one is happy all the time

☐ Stop expecting everybody to like you

☐ Don't expect people always to agree with you

☐ Stop expecting people to know what you're thinking

☐ Don't expect people to change

3 Read the article again. Which paragraphs should these people read and think about? There may be more than one possible answer.

1 'Billy's so unfriendly to me. I don't know what I've done wrong.'

2 'Can't they see I don't really feel like talking? I just want them to leave me alone.'

3 'Katie's always got a smile on her face. I wish my life was as perfect as hers.'

4 'I think Jenny would be a brilliant drummer for our band. I don't know what your problem is.'

5 'I wish Dylan wasn't so untidy. He always makes such a mess.'

4 SPEAKING Work in pairs. Discuss these questions.

1 Which piece of advice do you think is the best? Why?

2 What other advice would you add?

For a better life ...

Life can be hard, and when our plans don't work out, it's often easy to blame others. Sometimes we expect too much from friends and family, and when they don't act as we think they should, we feel disappointed. Maybe it would be easier if we stopped expecting so much from other people. No one is perfect, and that includes you.

1 _____

So you want to travel the world before you do a degree, but your parents don't think it's a good idea. Of course, it's great if other people can support you in your decisions, but you can't keep everyone happy all of the time. It's your life and you need to make the decisions to make you happy.

2 _____

Don't worry if there are people who aren't very nice to you, because there are plenty of people who are. They're called your friends. Spend time with them and avoid the others. And when it comes to finding that special person and settling down, remember: there's somebody for everyone.

3 _____

You've been practising football all summer. You think you're good enough to be in the school team, but the teacher doesn't seem to be thinking the same thing. Maybe he just hasn't thought about it at all. He isn't a mind reader, so tell him. Then at least he knows what you're thinking. He might even choose you.

4 _____

People can change, but they don't usually do it because someone else wants them to. You can try and tell them what you're not so happy about, so at least they know, but don't be too disappointed if they carry on doing exactly the same things. You have a choice: accept them or walk away.

5 _____

From their Facebook updates, you'd believe that all your friends are happy all the time and leading exciting lives. Of course, they aren't, just like you know that your life isn't always perfect. We all go through hard times and we often try to hide it. Be kind to people. They might be having a bad day and your smile could make a big difference.

VOCABULARY
Life plans

1 Match the phrases with the pictures.
Write 1–8 in the boxes.

1	retire	5	start a family
2	travel the world	6	settle down
3	start a career	7	get promoted
4	get a degree	8	leave school

2 Complete the text with phrases from Exercise 1.
Use the correct forms of the verbs.

My uncle has always done things differently. He
¹_____ when he was 16 because he wanted to see
other places. He spent the next twenty years
²_____, working in restaurants and hotels in many
different countries. When he was in his early forties, he
decided to return to the UK. He went to university and
³_____. He did really well, and when he finished, he
⁴_____ as a translator. Because he was good at his
job, he ⁵_____ quite quickly and he was soon Head
Translator. When he was 48, he met the love of his life
and they decided to ⁶_____ and ⁷_____ .
Now he's 55, with three young children. He says he wants
⁸_____ soon. He wants to stop working and take
the whole family around the world with him. I wouldn't be
surprised if he does.

Workbook page 12 ▶

■ THiNK SELF-ESTEEM ■

Life changes

1 Complete the table with your own ideas.

	One positive change	One negative change
You leave home	*Freedom*	*You have to look after yourself.*
You do a degree		
You start a career		
You start a family		
You get promoted		
You retire		

2 **SPEAKING** Work in small groups. Compare your ideas.

WRITING
An email about resolutions

Write an email to an English-speaking friend in another country. Describe your resolutions for the
coming school year. Write about:

• bad habits you're changing • new classes you're taking • activities you plan to take up • why you're doing all of this

What's up with Mia?

1 **Look at the photos and answer the questions.**

What do you think the problem is?
What does Mia want to give up?

2 🔊 1.10 **Now read and listen to the photostory. Check your answers.**

FLORA Hi, Leo. Hi, Jeff.
LEO Hi, Flora.
FLORA Hey, has either of you seen Mia lately?
JEFF No. I haven't seen her for ages, actually.
LEO Now you mention it, neither have I.
FLORA It's strange, isn't it? She hasn't been to the café for a long time. I wonder what she's up to.
LEO Hey, look who it is. Hi, Mia! We were just talking about you. Where have you been hiding?

1

2

MIA Don't even joke about it. I never have time to do anything any more.
FLORA Come and sit down. I'll get you something to drink.
MIA You're a star. That's just what I need.
JEFF So what's up, Mia? Why are you so busy?
MIA Where shall I start? Mondays, I have extra French lessons. Tuesdays, it's tennis lessons. Wednesdays, violin lessons. Thursdays, it's orchestra. Then every night I'm up late doing my homework.
LEO It's Thursday today.
MIA I know. I'm only here because orchestra was cancelled this week. Thank goodness.
LEO Don't you like playing the violin?
MIA Not really. I mean, I like playing an instrument. I just don't think I want to continue with the violin. Do you know I spend up to an hour every day practising?
FLORA So why do you do it?
MIA To keep my mum happy, I suppose.
JEFF You should talk to her, tell her you want to give it up.
MIA Yeah, maybe. But it's not always so easy to talk to her.
FLORA Well, you need to do something. You don't have any time for yourself. I mean, we never get to see you any more.
MIA Yeah, I guess you're right. It's up to me to do something about it.

THE FOLLOWING WEEK ...

3

CHLOE Hi, Mia.
MIA Hi, Chloë.
CHLOE What's up with you? You don't sound very happy.
MIA It's nothing.
CHLOE Really?
MIA Well, to be honest, I don't really feel like orchestra today.
CHLOE Why not?
MIA I haven't had any time to practise. And I'm tired. I don't know if I'm up to it.
CHLOE Don't be silly. I'm sure it'll be fine. Look, Mr Wales wants to start. Come on, Mia.
MIA Here we go. I am *not* looking forward to this.

DEVELOPING SPEAKING

3 Work in pairs. Discuss what you think Mia decides to do. Write down your ideas.

We think that Mia decides to carry on with the violin and continues playing in the orchestra.

4 ◀ EP1 Watch and find out how the story continues.

5 Answer the questions.

1 What happens at orchestra practice?
2 What reasons does Mia give to her mum for giving up the violin?
3 Why does Mia think her mum changed her mind?
4 How is Mia learning the guitar?
5 Why does Mia enjoy playing the guitar?

PHRASES FOR FLUENCY

1 Find these expressions in the photostory. Who says them? How do you say them in your language?

1 Now you mention it, …
2 Where have you been hiding?
3 You're a star.
4 Where shall I start?
5 Don't be silly.
6 Here we go.

2 Use the expressions in Exercise 1 to complete the conversations.

1 A You look tired. Has it been a busy day?
  B Busy? _____ First, I had a Maths test. Then I had Drama club at lunchtime. Then it was a five-kilometre run in PE …
  A Well, you just sit down and I'll get you something to eat.
  B Thanks, Mum. _____
2 A _____ , Annie? I haven't seen you for days.
  B I haven't been anywhere. You're the one who disappeared.
  A _____ , I have been quite busy.
3 A It's ten o'clock. Time for the test.
  B _____ I'm really not ready for this.
  A Me neither. I've got a feeling I'm not going to pass.
  B _____ You always pass.

WordWise
Phrases with *up*

1 Match the phrases in bold with the definitions.

1 So **what's up**, Mia?
2 Do you know I spend **up to** an hour every day practising?
3 I wonder what she's **up to**.
4 Then every night I'm **up** late doing my homework.
5 It's **up to me** to do something about it.
6 I don't know if I'm **up to** it.

a not in bed
b doing
c what's the matter?
d capable of
e as long as / to a maximum of
f my responsibility

2 Use words and phrases from Exercise 1 to complete the sentences.

1 What have you been _____ recently?
2 I was _____ late watching TV last night.
3 Oh, no! You look really unhappy. _____?
4 It isn't my decision. It's _____ you to decide.
5 He's 75 now, so he isn't _____ long walks.
6 This car can carry _____ six people.

Workbook page 12 ➜

Pronunciation
Linking words with *up*
Go to page 120. 🔊

FUNCTIONS
Complaining

1 Match the parts of the sentences.

1 I'm not happy with
2 The problem is that
3 He's always
4 If I'm honest, I don't

a it takes up so much time.
b picking on me.
c really like the violin.
d the way he talks to me.

2 ROLE PLAY Work in pairs. Student A: turn to page 127. Student B: turn to page 128.

OBJECTIVES

FUNCTIONS: talking about the past
GRAMMAR: narrative tenses (review); *would* and *used to*
VOCABULARY: descriptive verbs; time periods

READING

1 Look at the pictures and answer the questions.

1 What do the pictures illustrate?
2 How was life in the past harder than it is today?

2 Read the article quickly. Make notes on these questions about the Great Fire of London.

1	In what year did it happen?
2	How did it start?
3	How long did it last?
4	How did people get away?
5	How was the fire stopped?
6	What damage did it do?

3 🔊 1.13 **Read the article again and listen. Add details to your notes from Exercise 2.**

▮ TRAIN TO THiNK ▮▮▮

Following an idea through a paragraph

It can be difficult to follow what a writer is trying to say in a longer paragraph. We need to read carefully to understand fully what the writer is saying.

4 Answer the questions.

The end of Paragraph 2 says: 'The situation provided the perfect conditions for flames to spread quickly.'

1 Look back at the paragraph. How many things are needed to start a big fire? List them.
2 What were those things in London in 1666?

The beginning of Paragraph 3 says: 'The fire spread quickly but it was also extremely difficult to fight.'

3 Look back at the paragraph. Why was the fire difficult to fight?

The Great Fire of London
The event that changed the face of 17th-century London forever

It was 1 am on Sunday 2 September, 1666. London was sleeping. In a small bakery in Pudding Lane, Thomas Farriner and his workers were busily making bread for the coming day when, suddenly, a fire broke out. Just four days later, thousands of houses had been destroyed and countless people were homeless. How did this happen, and why was the damage so extensive?

For a fire to start, three things are needed: a spark, fuel and oxygen. In the bakery in Pudding Lane, a maid didn't tend to the ovens properly. They got too hot and sparks began to fly. The weather that year had been extremely hot. It hadn't rained for months. But people knew winter was coming, so they'd stocked their cupboards with food and oil. Warehouses were full of wood, coal and other winter supplies. A strong wind was blowing from the east. The situation provided the perfect conditions for flames to spread quickly. What followed was one of the biggest disasters of the 17th-century world.

The fire spread quickly, but it was also extremely difficult to fight. It started in a poor area of the city, where houses were built very close to one another. Tens of thousands of people were living in very small spaces. A simple house was often home to many families as well as lodgers. As the catastrophe struck, people panicked. Some had to smash their doors to get out of their homes. The streets were blocked with people and with material that had fallen from houses. Many people had grabbed their most important possessions and were trying to flee from the flames with them. They screamed in terror and suffered from the heat and the smoke. Some escaped from the city on boats. Others simply dived into the river to save themselves.

The fire had been raging for almost four days when the Duke of York put a plan into action. His soldiers demolished a large warehouse full of paper. This robbed the fire of more fuel and created a 'fire break' that the flames could not jump over. At about this time, the wind also changed direction, driving the fire back into itself. At last, the flames died down enough to be controlled. The fire was finished.

Although surprisingly few people lost their lives, at least 13,000 houses – 80 per cent of the city's buildings – had been destroyed. Thousands of people had become homeless and had lost everything they owned. Gradually, houses were rebuilt in the ruins, but this took several years. Many Londoners moved away from their city and never returned.

SPEAKING

Work in pairs. Discuss these questions.

1 What other events would you suggest for the *Events that shook the world* series? Why?
2 If you had to leave your home in a hurry and had the time to save three things, what would you choose?

GRAMMAR
Narrative tenses (review)

1 **Match the sentences from the article on page 21 with the tenses. Then complete the rule.**

1 London **was sleeping**.
2 Thomas Farriner and his workers **were** busily **making** bread […] when, suddenly, a fire broke out.
3 It **hadn't rained** for months.
4 The fire **had been raging** for almost four days.
5 His soldiers **demolished** a large warehouse.

a past perfect
b past simple
c past continuous (two sentences)
d past perfect continuous

> **RULE:**
> **We use …**
> 1 _____ to talk about finished actions in the past.
> 2 _____ to talk about longer actions in the past interrupted by shorter actions.
> 3 _____ to set the scene.
> 4 _____ to talk about actions before a certain time in the past.
> 5 _____ to talk about uninterrupted actions before a certain time in the past.

2 **Complete the sentences with the past simple or past continuous form of the verbs.**

0 While people *were running* towards the river, a warehouse *exploded* . (run / explode)
1 When they _____ how serious the situation was, they _____ their possessions and _____ to get away. (notice / take / try)
2 A man _____ for his family when he _____ a baby in the street. (look / find)
3 While they _____ how to stop the fire, it _____ clear that little could be done. (think / become)
4 While the people in the bakery _____ bread, a small fire _____ . (make / start)

3 **Complete the conversation with the correct form of the verbs. Use the tenses from Exercise 1.**

burn | do | see | run | sit | walk | go | open

IAN   I had a real scare yesterday. As I ¹_____ up to our house, I ²_____ smoke coming from the window.
OLI   ³_____ something _____?
IAN   Fortunately not. I ⁴_____ into the house, ⁵_____ the kitchen door and there was my brother. He ⁶_____ on the floor in shock. He ⁷_____ science experiments! One of them ⁸_____ wrong and exploded.

Workbook page 18

VOCABULARY
Descriptive verbs

1 **Certain verbs make narratives sound more dramatic. Find these words in a dictionary and write down:**

1 what they mean.
2 their past simple and past participle forms.

smash | rage | dive | flee | strike
demolish | grab | scream

2 **Replace the underlined words with words from Exercise 1. Change the form if necessary.**

0 He picked up a stone and <u>broke</u> the windscreen of the car.   *smashed*
1 The thief stole a motorbike and <u>escaped</u>.   _____
2 The fires had been <u>burning</u> for days, and no one knew how to stop them.   _____
3 When I got there, I heard somebody <u>shouting</u> with fear.   _____
4 They <u>knocked down</u> the houses to make space for new shops.   _____
5 The man <u>took</u> my wallet <u>from me quickly</u> and ran away.   _____
6 The car lost control and <u>hit</u> another vehicle.   _____
7 He took off his clothes and <u>jumped</u> into the water.   _____

Workbook page 20

> ## Pronunciation
> Initial consonant clusters with /s/
> **Go to page 120.**

LISTENING

1 Look at the picture. Why do you think the cow was in court? Choose the best option.

A It was accused of killing a human.

B It was interrupting a court meeting.

C A man was accused of hurting the cow.

2 🔊 1.16 Listen to Ryan's talk. Then answer the questions.

1 When were animals taken to court?

2 In which parts of the world did this happen?

3 🔊 1.16 Listen again. For questions 1–5, choose A, B or C.

1 What were the French rats accused of?

A entering restaurants

B taking people's food

C hunting cats

2 According to the man, why didn't the rats accept their order to appear in court?

A They hadn't received it.

B They couldn't read it.

C They'd never accept an invitation from humans.

3 Why did he say the rats would never go to court?

A No one would understand them.

B They might not be safe.

C They couldn't be friends with humans.

4 How did the other people react to the man?

A They thought he was crazy.

B They laughed at him.

C They couldn't argue against him.

5 What happened to the rats?

A They were hunted and killed.

B They were found 'not guilty'.

C They were ordered to leave the village.

▌THiNK VALUES ▌

Animal rights

1 Read the scenarios. Match them with statements 1–6. There are two statements for each scenario.

Scenario A: ☐ / ☐

Work on a huge multi-million-pound shopping centre has been stopped because nests of an extremely rare frog have been found in the area. It is one of only five places where this frog breeds. The property developers are putting pressure on the local government, saying it will be a disaster for the economy if they aren't allowed to finish the job.

Scenario B: ☐ / ☐

An elderly lady lives on her own. She has family, but they all live far away. A relative has suggested buying her a parrot for her 80th birthday. Other family members are against the idea of keeping an animal in a cage.

Scenario C: ☐ / ☐

There is a hotel that's very popular with tourists because it's close to a beautiful forest. The forest is home to a species of large spider. Although it's harmless, people working in the hotel have been given strict orders to kill any spiders that get into the guest rooms.

1 A bird in a cage can be a great companion for a person who lives alone, so it's the right present.

2 Creating places where people can relax is more important than worrying about a few animals.

3 We can't afford to lose any species of animal.

4 Places where endangered animals have their natural habitat belong to the animals, and not to people.

5 Spiders are ugly and disgusting, and many people are scared of them. Of course they should be killed.

6 Birds need to fly, and they need space to be able to do that. Cages should be forbidden.

2 SPEAKING Which of the statements 1–6 do you agree and disagree with? Why? Make notes of your answers. Then compare your ideas in pairs or small groups.

READING

1   Work in pairs. Look at the pictures, the main title and the paragraph titles. What information do you think each paragraph might contain?

2   Read the article and check your answers.

Family life
in 17th-century Britain

By the 17th century, life in Europe had started to become more comfortable for those who had money. Trade had become more important, and the number of people who could read and write was starting to grow. But while the rich were enjoying good food, poetry and the theatre, life for the poor hadn't changed much at all. Here are a few examples of what ordinary family life was like in the olden days.

A typical household

Women used to have seven or eight children, but one in every three children died before reaching one year of age. Many children had

to leave home when they were as young as seven years old to work as shepherds or helpers on farms. There weren't many elderly people in the families because people died much younger than they usually do today. Few people expected to live beyond 40. In fact, children frequently grew up without parents at all.

A crowded life

Ordinary people used to live in one-room houses, together with chickens, goats or even cows. Only richer families had mattresses. On cold nights, everyone in the family would crowd together to sleep, to warm each other up. Unfortunately, this had a bad effect on people's health. Lice infestations were very common, and if one person suffered from an illness, everybody else would get it

too. Taking a bath was such a rare event that everybody smelled bad.

Childcare

Life didn't allow people to spend a lot of time with their children. Parents used to leave even very young children on their own for most of the day. Records from that time report many stories of children who got too close to the fire and burned to death. But even when parents were with their children, they didn't care for them in the ways we're used to parents doing today. Children were often simply considered workers. Parents didn't use to sing songs to their children or play with them. It used to be normal to call a child 'it' rather than 'he' or 'she'.

It's often easy to fantasise about the past and think how wonderfully simple life was compared to all the pressure we face in our day-to-day lives. But was it really so great? For most people, it probably wasn't.

3   Read the article again. Mark the sentences T (true) or F (false). Correct the false sentences.

1   Life in the 17th century was difficult for everybody, no matter how much money they had. ☐

2   Grandparents often used to live with the families and look after the young children. ☐

3   There wasn't a lot of space in most people's homes and they often shared it with their animals. ☐

4   Children sometimes died because their parents weren't very concerned about their safety. ☐

5   Parents these days spend more time with their children than they did in the olden days. ☐

4   **SPEAKING** Work in pairs. Discuss these questions.

1   Compare family life in the 17th century with family life now. What are the most striking differences?

2   What do you think life will be like 100 years from now? Will it be easier? If so, how?

GRAMMAR
would and *used to*

1 **Complete these sentences from the article on page 24. Then complete the rule with *used to / didn't use to* and *would(n't)*.**

1 Women _____ have seven or eight children.

2 On cold nights, everyone in the family _____ crowd together to sleep, to warm each other up.

3 Parents _____ sing songs to their children or play with them.

4 It _____ be normal to call a child 'it' rather than 'he' or 'she'.

> **RULE:** To talk about habits and repeated actions in the past, we can use *used to / didn't use to* or *would(n't)*.
> - We use [1]_____ with both action and stative verbs.
> - We only use [2]_____ with action verbs.

2 **Circle the correct words. Sometimes both options are possible.**

1 When I was a child, I *would / used to* play a lot with my sister.

2 We *would / used to* have a cat, Tubby.

3 We *would / used to* like her a lot and play with her all the time.

4 It's funny, but I *would / used to* think I'd never learn to read.

5 We *would / used to* share a bedroom.

6 My sister and I *would / used to* be such good friends!

3 **Complete the sentences and conversations with the correct form of *used to*.**

1 A _____ you _____ have a pet when you were a child?

   B Yes, I _____ have a cat.

2 We _____ have a car. We used to walk everywhere.

3 A _____ you _____ watch a lot of TV when you were younger?

   B Yes, I _____ watch it every day when I got home from school.

4 I _____ like vegetables, but I love them now.

5 A _____ your dad _____ read you stories before you went to bed?

   B No, he didn't, but my mum _____ .

6 I _____ like having birthday parties. I was a really shy child.

Workbook page 19

VOCABULARY
Time periods

Look at phrases 1–9 and match them with categories a–c. Compare your answers with the class.

a the present

b the recent past

c a long, long time ago in history

1 from 1995 until 2004

2 in the Middle Ages

3 in this day and age

4 these days

5 in the olden days

6 in the last century

7 not so long ago

8 a decade ago

9 nowadays

Workbook page 20

FUNCTIONS
Talking about the past

Work in pairs. Choose a topic for your partner and a period in the past. Your partner makes a comparison between the present and that time period. Take turns.

school | food | technology
games | home | travel

games in the 1930s

Well, children would play with teddy bears or dolls. These days, many children have electronic games.

Culture

1 **Look at the photos and answer the questions.**

1 In what part of the world were these photos taken?

2 Why might life be difficult there? How many reasons can you think of?

2 🔊 1.17 **Read and listen to the article. Check your predictions.**

Where life is really hard

It's the end of the winter. Most people have been inside for weeks. They haven't seen the sun for a long time. But some men are outside. It's bitterly cold, with temperatures of around -45° Celsius, and the freezing wind makes the situation difficult for them to bear. These men are hunters, and the survival of the people they've left behind in the villages depends on how successful their hunt is.

Akycha is one of these men. He's been out hunting for more than a week now. While he's away from home, he stays overnight in a little igloo that he's made himself from ice and snow. The igloo protects him from the freezing wind. Inside, there's a little stove for cooking, and a small stone lamp which provides light. Together, they help to create a temperature of around 12° Celsius.

Right now, Akycha is several kilometres away from his igloo. He's riding his snowmobile along the coast, far out on the frozen sea. Suddenly, he can see something in the distance. He stops his snowmobile and checks through his binoculars. It's a seal. Holding a screen of white canvas in front of him in one hand, and his gun in the other, he moves forward, cautiously hiding behind the screen all the time so that the seal won't notice him. If he's lucky and his hunt goes well, the meat he brings home should last his family for several weeks.

Akycha and his people are part of the Inuit community. Most of them still live a very traditional life, a life that makes them dependent on hunting seals and whales. Some of them also live off the reindeer they keep.

The Inuit are indigenous people of the Arctic Circle, which means they've lived here for so long that they feel the land is theirs. The Arctic Circle is a huge land area that belongs to a number of northern countries: Russia, the USA, Canada, Greenland, Norway, Sweden, Finland and Iceland. The northern environment is an exceptional habitat. Temperatures are low during most of the year and summers are short, which means that plants can only grow for a few weeks every year. If the reindeer eat the moss that grows in a certain area, it can take up to 30 years for the plants to grow back. This is why Inuits who make a living from keeping and breeding reindeer have to be constantly on the move with their herds.

For most of us, life is less hard than it is for the Inuit people. But maybe we can learn something from them. Their traditional way of life is a model of living in partnership with nature, rather than exploiting and destroying it.

3 **Read the article again. Answer the questions.**

1 What are winters like inside the Arctic Circle?

2 How does Akycha survive when he's out hunting?

3 What does he hunt and how does he do this?

4 Why can't the Inuit who keep reindeer stay in one place for a long time?

4 **SPEAKING** **Work in pairs. Discuss these questions.**

1 In what other areas of the world do people live under extreme conditions?

2 What is the coldest or hottest place you've ever been in? What was the experience like for you?

3 Would you find it easier to live in an area where it's very cold or very hot?

5 VOCABULARY There are eight highlighted words or phrases in the article. Match them with these definitions.

1 continue to be enough
2 not taken with them
3 from one evening, through to the next morning
4 not staying in one place for very long
5 tolerate, put up with
6 large groups of animals
7 a type of plant
8 raising (animals)

WRITING

A magazine article about a historical event

1 Read the article. What happened in Berlin in these years?

1 1961   2 1989   3 1990

2 Find examples in the article of:

1 a sentence containing the past simple and the past continuous.
2 the past perfect.
3 the past perfect continuous.
4 descriptive verbs.
5 expressions referring back to the past.

3 The article has three paragraphs. Which of them:

1 sets the scene for the main events?
2 describes the main action?
3 describes the historical background?

4 Think of an event that shook the world.

• Do some Internet research to find out more about it.
• Choose the most important and interesting details.
• Organise the information into paragraphs.
• Think about the language you'll need to describe the event.

5 Write an article for a school magazine about an event that shook the world (200 words).

The fall of the Berlin Wall

For 28 years, Berlin was a divided city. Ever since its construction in 1961, a huge wall had stopped citizens from East Germany visiting their neighbours in the west. Many people had tried. Some were successful, but many more died, shot as they attempted to get to the other side.

In 1989, there were a number of radical political demonstrations across Eastern Europe, as the people of countries such as Poland and Hungary protested against their governments and managed to change them. On 9 November, the East German government announced that their people were free to visit the western side of the city.

That evening, thousands of East Berliners rushed to the wall and demanded that the gates were opened. The border guards didn't know what to do. While the crowds were singing, the guards phoned their bosses for orders. It soon became clear that they had no choice but to let the people pass. On the other side, the crowds were greeted by West Berliners with flowers and champagne. People climbed up onto the top of the wall and began dancing on it to celebrate their new freedom. People started arriving with sledgehammers to try and smash down the wall. Many grabbed bricks as souvenirs. A little later, the government sent in bulldozers to demolish the wall. The wall that had been dividing a city for nearly three decades was soon gone and, 339 days later, the two nations of East and West Germany also became one.

READING AND USE OF ENGLISH
Part 1: Multiple-choice cloze

Workbook page 17

1 For questions 1–8, read the text below and decide which answer (A, B, C or D) best fits each gap. There is an example at the beginning (0).

0   A (stopped)   B   finished   C   ended   D   not

Do you ever stop and think about how easy the Internet has made our lives? I know there are times when it's slow or has **(0)** ___ working altogether, times when maybe you feel like **(1)** ___ your computer screen into tiny pieces. But just think of all those things you use it for. You want to buy the new One Direction CD – you can **(2)** ___ online and buy it. You need to **(3)** ___ some research for your homework – you can find it all there on the web. You feel like a **(4)** ___ with your best friend, so you Skype them. You just want a **(5)** ___ from your homework, so you start up Minecraft or whatever game it is you prefer and start playing. These **(6)** ___ everything we need is just a click of a button away.

Of course, it wasn't always like this. Only a few decades **(7)** ___ , people had to do things like go to the shops if they wanted to buy something and often those shops were closed! They had to look in very large, heavy books called encyclopedias to find information. They had to **(8)** ___ up the telephone if they wanted to talk and if their best friend wasn't at home, they simply couldn't talk to them. That's how tough life was. And these poor people who had to suffer such hardships were … our parents! Makes you feel sorry for them, doesn't it?

1	A demolishing	B	striking	C smashing	D	grabbing
2	A come	B	enter	C click	D	go
3	A do	B	make	C find	D	ask
4	A talking	B	chat	C question	D	speak
5	A break	B	stop	C end	D	fix
6	A times	B	ages	C years	D	days
7	A after	B	since	C ago	D	past
8	A take	B	pick	C grab	D	hold

SPEAKING
Part 1: Interview

Workbook page 25

2 In pairs, ask and answer the questions.

1   Who do you spend the most time with at the weekends, and what do you do with them?
2   What kind of films do you like best? What do you like about them?
3   Where did you go for your last holiday? What was it like?
4   What's your favourite sport to play? What do you like about it?
5   What things do you enjoy doing the most with your parents?
6   What is your favourite room in your home and why do you like it?
7   If you could be anywhere now, where would it be and why?
8   What things do you like to do at home on a rainy day?
9   Who is your best friend and what do you like the most about him/her?

TEST YOURSELF UNITS 1 & 2

VOCABULARY

1 Complete the sentences with the words in the list. There are four extra words.

break | change | do | form | give up | grab | make
scream | retire | settle | smash | strike | struggle | travel

1 It would be wonderful to _____ around the world one day.
2 It's a really bad habit – I need to _____ it soon.
3 He would always arrive late, and no one could make him _____ his ways.
4 Good luck with the test – I'm sure you'll _____ really well.
5 Every 31st December, I _____ a resolution to do something, but I usually break it!
6 I saw a man _____ that woman's purse and run away.
7 On her 65th birthday, she decided to _____ and travel the world.
8 I need more time to study for my exams, so I'm going to _____ my judo classes for a while.
9 I think he's going to break the record – in fact, he's going to _____ it!
10 They were so excited by the concert that they started to _____ really loudly.   `/10`

GRAMMAR

2 Complete the sentences with the phrases in the list. There are two extra phrases.

was looking | would look | 'm seeing | are going to | go to | used to love | see | 'll love

1 I _____ my aunt and uncle once a month.
2 Four or five of us _____ eat pizza tonight.
3 Have fun at the concert – I'm sure you _____ it!
4 When I was a kid, I _____ going to the river to swim.
5 I'm not very well, so I _____ the doctor tomorrow.
6 When I saw her, she _____ in a shop window.

3 Find and correct the mistake in each sentence.

1 When he was young, my dad used to reading books about nature.
2 When I got to the house, there was no one there. The party finished!
3 I am running in the park every morning before school.
4 We're really excited because we will go on holiday next week.
5 He was tired because he had been running two kilometres.
6 While I was cycling in the park, I was falling off my bicycle.   `/12`

FUNCTIONAL LANGUAGE

4 Circle the correct words.

1 A I'm angry with Jack. He's *always / often* picking on me.
   B I know. He's horrible. *I don't like / I'm not liking* him at all.
2 A You know, in the *past / olden* days, people didn't have the Internet.
   B I know! But *these days / not so long ago* we can get information so quickly!
3 A Gina and I *have / are having* lunch tomorrow. Why don't you come too?
   B Great – thank you! *I see / I'll see* you at the restaurant!   `/8`
4 A No one *uses / is using* typewriters any more.
   B Not in *nowadays / this day and age*, no!

MY SCORE `/30`

| 22 – 30 |
| 10 – 21 |
| 0 – 9 |

29

3 WHAT'S IN A NAME?

READING

1 **Look at the names and logos and answer the questions.**

   1 These are the names and logos of various companies. What kind of products do they offer?

   > *Jaguar sells cars.*

   2 Add two more names of companies or products that are famous around the world.

2 **SPEAKING** Work in pairs. Some people think the name of a brand is very important. What do you think is the reason for this?

3 Read the blog entry quickly. Which of the brands shown above does it mention?

4 🔊 1.18 **Read the blog entry again and listen. Answer the questions.**

   1 Why do companies think a lot about a brand name?
   2 What makes a good brand name?
   3 Why were each of these names chosen?
      Jaguar | Pret A Manger | WhatsApp
   4 Why was Nova a bad name for a car in Spain?
   5 Why do some teenagers choose to buy more expensive products (like clothes)?

▌ TRAIN TO THINK ▌

Identifying the main topic of a paragraph

Writers use a new paragraph when they want to change the topic. The opening line of a paragraph usually gives you a clue about its topic.

5 **Look at paragraphs 3 and 4. What is the topic of each paragraph? Tick (✓) two options.**

   A what teenagers wear to school ☐
   B brand names are important in the teenage market ☐
   C some really bad brand names ☐
   D ways to pick a brand name ☐

Brand names

1 OK, so imagine you've thought of a great idea for a product to make and sell – a game, or an app, or some clothes, for example. You know you can sell millions of them, but first of all, you must give the product a name – a brand name. And that may not be as easy as you think.

2 The brand name is the thing that distinguishes your product from all the others, and it's really important that it makes an impact. Businesses spend a lot of time thinking about brand names; when the name has been picked, it's very difficult to change, so companies have to get it right first time.

3 So how do you choose a name? A brand name ought to be unique, memorable and easy to understand. It should create some kind of emotional connection with people who buy the product – the target market. Some companies use the family name. When Henry Ford started making cars, he just called the company Ford. But you don't have to use a family name – you can go for an image. Staying with cars, think about the brand name Jaguar, a beautiful but dangerous wild cat. What does that say about the manufacturer's product? Some companies use wordplay. It's a common technique for naming apps, for example WhatsApp (from the English expression What's up?). Others like to use foreign words because they sound special or different. For example, in Britain and the USA there's a chain of sandwich shops with the French name Pret A Manger, which means 'ready to eat'. And what do you have to be careful about? Well, you shouldn't choose a name that might not work in certain countries or cultures.

Many years ago, a car company launched a new car that they called Nova. They thought it suggested something nice and new, but in Spanish it can be read as no va ('it doesn't go'). Not a good name for a car in Spain, then!

4 These days, the choice of brand name is particularly important if your product is targeted at the teenage market. Teenage consumers are perhaps more concerned with brand names and company logos than any other group. When a brand, especially a clothing brand, becomes popular with teenagers, then there's a lot of pressure to wear those clothes and have the name and/or logo visible. A teacher in an American high school said: 'I certainly see that kids are obsessed with brand names. They won't buy something that's almost identical – and cheaper – simply because they feel they must wear something with the right logo.' So if you want to get into the teenage market, you have to find a product and a brand name that works with that age group, and create some great advertisements too.

5 Companies know that the name isn't everything – the product itself has to be good, of course – but it's an essential part of the package.

'I'm so glad that we don't have to wear school uniforms any more!'

SPEAKING

Work in pairs. Discuss these questions.

1 Can you think of any more brand names which:
   a use a family name?
   b try to create an image?
   c are in another language?

2 Have you ever bought or wanted something just because of the brand? Give examples.

GRAMMAR

(don't) have to / ought to / should(n't) / must

1 Complete the sentences from the article on page 31. Then complete the rule with *have to*, *don't have to*, *ought to*, *should*, *shouldn't* and *must*.

1 First of all, you _____ give the product a name.
2 Companies _____ get it right first time.
3 A brand name _____ be unique, memorable and easy to understand.
4 But you _____ use a family name.
5 And what _____ you _____ be careful about?
6 Well, you _____ choose a name that might not work in certain countries or cultures.

> **RULE:** We use [1]_____ or _____ to say 'this is important or necessary'. We use [2]_____ to say 'this isn't important or necessary'. We use [3]_____ or _____ to tell someone that something is a good idea. We use [4]_____ to tell someone that something isn't a good idea. (*Ought to* isn't as frequent as *should*. It is used mostly in writing, and the negative form is rare.)

2 Complete the conversation with the correct form of *have to*.

MANDY   Mum, there's a new mobile phone out. It's brilliant. I [1]_____ get one!
MUM   No way! Your mobile phone is fine. You [2]_____ buy another one.
MANDY   But you know what it's like at school. Everyone [3]_____ have the latest product!
MUM   Yes, and it's terrible. Why [4]_____ you all _____ wear the same clothes, for example?
MANDY   Because it's what teenagers do. You were young once. Don't you remember?
MUM   I see. And I [5]_____ go to work to pay for all these things, right?
MANDY   Oh, Mum! You [6]_____ be difficult!

3 Complete the conversation with suitable modal verbs. There is often more than one possible answer.

GILL   The new café is great – you[1]_____ go there.
JACK   I've heard it's a bit expensive.
GILL   Yes, that's true. You [2]_____ go there every day. But you [3]_____ try the cakes – they're delicious!
JACK   OK. What's the place called, anyway?
GILL   Can you believe it's called The Coffee Shop?!
JACK   What a boring name! You [4]_____ be a genius to think of that!
GILL   They [5]_____ have a foreign name, like Le Café.
JACK   Well, OK. But it [6]_____ be easy to pronounce. There's a shop in town called Arighi Bianchi and no one knows how to say it.
GILL   But the owner is Italian. It's his name!
JACK   I guess I [7]_____ know that. Anyway, I [8]_____ go home and do my homework for tomorrow.
GILL   You [9]_____ worry about that. It's easy.
JACK   Really? OK, so let's go to the cinema. There's a new film that we [10]_____ see!

Workbook page 28

VOCABULARY
Making and selling

1 Complete the sentences with the words.

advertisement | brand | chain | consumers image | logo | manufacturer | products

1 They make cleaning _____, like washing powder.
2 The prices have gone up a lot, so now _____ have to pay more.
3 I always buy the same _____ of shoes – they're so comfortable.
4 It's a _____ that has shops in every town.
5 That shop has a really funny _____ on TV.
6 The Nike _____ is a large tick.
7 When the company's director went to prison it damaged the company's _____ .
8 If it doesn't work, send it back to the _____ .

2 **SPEAKING** Answer the questions. Then work in pairs and compare your answers.

Can you name …

1 three places where you find advertisements?
2 a manufacturer of mobile phones?
3 a chain of shops and a chain of restaurants?
4 one thing you always buy the same brand of?

Workbook page 30

LISTENING

1 ◀)) 1.19 **Listen to Paul talking to his teacher, Mrs Jenkins. What is their conversation about? (Circle) the correct option.**

A how to remember names
B why some names are hard to remember
C why some people can't remember names

2 ◀)) 1.19 **Listen again. Mark the sentences T (true) or F (false).**

1 Mrs Jenkins has taught Paul's class three times. ☐
2 Paul isn't good at remembering people's names. ☐
3 Mrs Jenkins says you have to concentrate if you want to remember names. ☐
4 Mrs Jenkins thinks it's useful to say the person's name as soon as you hear it. ☐
5 She remembered Paul's name because she knows another person called Paul. ☐
6 She always remembers people's names. ☐

GRAMMAR
had better (not)

1 **Complete these sentences from the listening. Then (circle) the correct words to complete the rule.**

1 I _____ go now.
2 You _____ be late for your next class.

> **RULE:** We use *had ('d) better* to warn someone that bad things will happen if they ¹*do / don't do* something. We use *had ('d) better not* to warn someone that bad things will happen if they ²*do / don't do* something.

2 **Complete the sentences with *had better (not)*.**

1 The bus goes in two minutes. You _____ run.
2 I'll lend you my pen – but you _____ break it!
3 It's going to rain. We _____ go inside.
4 You have to get up very early tomorrow, so you _____ go to bed. It's 1 am.
5 You _____ eat any more sweets. You'll be sick.

Workbook page 29 ▶

FUNCTIONS
Giving advice

1 ◀)) 1.20 **Put the sentences in the correct order to make two conversations. Then listen and check.**

1 ☐ LIAM Why? What's her name?
   ☐ LIAM What's the matter, Jo?
   ☐ LIAM Well, you'd better get some help – quickly!
   ☐ JO It's something like Sharita Wass Ikonor.
   ☐ JO I've got to phone someone and I've no idea how to pronounce her name.

2 ☐ BOB Well, I wrote the wrong name in my birthday card to her son. I called him Jason, not Jacob.
   ☐ BOB I know. She's really cross.
   ☐ BOB My sister's really angry with me.
   ☐ MIA Why?
   ☐ MIA You'd better not do that again!

2 **Work in pairs. Imagine you forgot your best friend's birthday. Write a conversation using *had better (not)*.**

▌THiNK SELF-ESTEEM ▌
People and their names

1 **Complete the questionnaire (1 = I strongly agree; 5 = I strongly disagree).**

1 I find it easy to remember people's names. ☐
2 I only remember the names of people I like. ☐
3 I hate it when people forget my name. ☐
4 Your name is an important part of who you are. ☐
5 I feel sorry for people who have unusual names. ☐

2 **SPEAKING Compare your answers in small groups. Which question(s) do you agree on?**

READING

1 Look at the names and answer the questions.

Apple Martin | Brooklyn Beckham | Moon Unit Zappa

1 Do you know anything about these people?

2 Think of one thing that they have in common.

2 These are eight names that parents tried to call their children. Which do you think were allowed (✓) or not allowed (✗) by the government?

☐ 1 Talula does the Hula from Hawaii

☐ 2 Fish and Chips

☐ 3 Number 16 Bus Shelter

☐ 4 Google

☐ 5 Ikea

☐ 6 Q

☐ 7 Pluto

☐ 8 Monkey

Brooklyn Beckham

Moon Unit Zappa

3 Read the article and check your answers to Exercise 2.

4 Read the article again. Answer the questions.

1 Which people's unusual names do we often hear about?

2 What reason did a New Zealand judge give for not allowing some names?

3 What did Mariléia dos Santos decide to do?

4 What did she become well known for?

5 Why did David Carradine give his son an unusual name?

5 SPEAKING Mark each statement with a number from 1 to 5 (1 = I strongly agree; 5 = I strongly disagree).

a Parents should be able to give their children any name they want.

b Children with silly names should be allowed to change them when they're 12 years old.

c It doesn't matter what name a child has because they can change it as an adult.

d Every country should have a list of names that parents are allowed to give their children.

6 SPEAKING Compare your answers with other people in the class.

Crazy names

Names for your children: it's always a big question for parents. Should you give them an 'ordinary' name or do you want something a bit different? We always hear about big names in the world of cinema, music or sport who prefer something that isn't ordinary. And so they give their kids names like Apple or Brooklyn or Moon Unit. Other people like to use brand names for their children, so there are now quite a few people called Armani or Diesel running around in school playgrounds.

So can you call your child anything you want? Well, it depends where you live. In New Zealand, for example, you can't call your child Talula Does The Hula From Hawaii, and you can't call your twins Fish and Chips. (And yes, parents in New Zealand really have tried to give their kids these names.)

It's hard to believe, but you can call a child Number 16 Bus Shelter. Generally, certain names aren't allowed because, as a New Zealand judge said in one case, 'a name mustn't make a fool of the child'. In Sweden, if you want the name Google for your kid, then go ahead – no problem. But you'd better not try to call your children Ikea or Q, because the government won't let you. Things are even more difficult in Denmark. There's an official list of about 7,000 approved names, and parents need special permission to use a name that isn't on it. Pluto and Monkey didn't get on it.

Of course, when kids grow up, they can decide to change their name, and then it's a different game altogether. If a woman footballer wants to call herself Michael Jackson, which is what Brazilian player Mariléia dos Santos decided to do, then there's nothing to stop her. (She made a name for herself as one of the best female footballers in the world.) And, of course, singers do it all the time. Shawn Corey Carter and Stefani Germanotta, for example, might not be household names today if they hadn't decided to use the stage names Jay-Z and Lady Gaga. Some people, however, change their name from something unusual to something ordinary in order to blend in. David Carradine named his son Free because he wanted him to feel free to do anything, even to change his name – which he did, to Tom.

GRAMMAR
can('t) / must(n't)

1 **Complete these sentences from the listening on page 33 and the article on page 34. Then complete the rule with *can*, *can't* and *mustn't*.**

1 _____ I ask you something?

2 You _____ call your twins Fish and Chips.

3 You _____ call a child Number 16 Bus Shelter.

4 A name '_____ make a fool of the child'.

> **RULE:** To talk or ask about permission, we often use the modal verb [1]_____ . To say what isn't allowed, we often use [2]_____ or _____ .

2 **Complete the sentences with *mustn't* and the verbs. Then match them with the pictures.**

run | talk | be | miss

1 You _____ so loudly!

2 I _____ be late.

3 I _____ the goal!

4 You _____ .

3 **Rewrite the sentences using modal verbs from this unit and the pronouns in brackets. There is often more than one possible answer.**

0 Diving isn't allowed. (you) *You can't dive here.*

1 It isn't necessary for us to wear uniforms. (we)

2 It's a good idea to buy a new phone. (you)

3 It's OK for you to use my laptop. (you)

4 It's necessary for them to work harder. (they)

5 Are we allowed to play here? (we)

Workbook page 29

VOCABULARY
Expressions with *name*

1 **Match the <u>underlined</u> expressions with the definitions.**

1 Tony Hawk is <u>a big name</u> in skateboarding.

2 He's upset because some of the other kids <u>call him names</u>.

3 Jay-Z isn't his real name – it's his <u>stage name</u>.

4 Fish, meat, vegetables, fruit – <u>you name it</u>, I eat it.

5 Look! It's <u>what's-his-name / what's-her-name</u>.

6 We want to get married, but we haven't <u>named the day</u> yet.

7 I know you don't want to do the exams, but it's <u>the name of the game</u> for university entry.

8 He <u>made a name for himself</u> as a great actor.

a decide the date of an event, often a wedding

b someone whose name I can't remember

c the most important part of something

d a person who is important or famous in their profession

e a name that a person (usually an actor or a singer) uses in their profession

f use rude names about, or to, a person

g become known or respected by many people

h anything you say (or choose)

2 **Complete the missing word(s).**

1 She's been to Europe, Asia and Australia – you _____ _____ , she's been there!

2 Hard work is the _____ of _____ _____ if you want to do well in your exams.

3 My uncle's a doctor. He's a _____ _____ in the field of cancer research.

4 Some of her classmates _____ her _____ . It's horrible for her.

5 You're engaged? That's wonderful! When are you going to _____ _____ day?

6 Oh look! There's _____-his-_____ – you know, that boy who lives in your street.

7 She made _____ _____ for _____ on a reality TV show and became a famous singer.

8 Bruno Mars is the _____ name of Pete Gene Hernandez.

Workbook page 30

> **Pronunciation**
> **Strong and weak forms: /ɒv/ and /əv/**
> **Go to page 120.**

Fiction

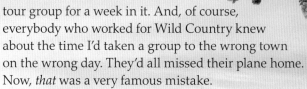

1 🔊 **1.23** Read and listen to the introduction and the first part of the extract. Answer the questions.

1 What is Tess's full name?
2 In the company, her name is used to mean something. What, and why?

Wild Country by Margaret Johnson

Tess and Grant are tour leaders for a group walking holiday in France. But they don't get on well – at least at the start …

'I didn't ask to work with you,' Grant said, 'and I know you didn't ask to work with me. But here we are, so shall we at least try to get on with each other?' I looked back at him crossly. 'I'll try if you try,' I said, but I didn't like the smile he gave me.

I'd been a tour leader for Wild Country, my father's walking holiday company, for a year. In that time I'd been late meeting a group at the airport several times. I'd also lost my wallet, with all the money to buy food for the tour group for a week in it. And, of course, everybody who worked for Wild Country knew about the time I'd taken a group to the wrong town on the wrong day. They'd all missed their plane home. Now, *that* was a very famous mistake.

My mistakes were so famous in the company that doing something wrong was called 'doing a Tess Marriot'. I think it was Grant Cooper who started saying that, actually – horrible man.

2 🔊 **1.24** Read and listen to the second part of the extract. Mark the sentences T (true) or F (false).

1 Tess thinks her father's idea was a bad one. ☐
2 She's happy when she arrives at the airport. ☐
3 She tries hard to smile when she goes into the airport. ☐
4 She likes Grant because he laughs a lot. ☐
5 She helps Grant to find the group of tourists. ☐

And now my father had arranged for me to work with Grant Cooper on this tour. He thought I would learn something from Grant — something to make me a better tour leader. I thought my father was wrong. I was just too different to Grant; and I didn't *want* to be like him anyway.

After thirty minutes in a hot bus with these thoughts going round and round my head I felt very fed up. Which was the opposite of how I should be when I meet a group at the start of a holiday.

'A tour leader should smile as often as possible.' That's what it said in the book I was given when I started the job. 'At the beginning of a tour, holidaymakers are often tired from their journeys. They may also be worried about what the other people on the holiday will be like. A smile from you makes everybody feel better.'

So as I entered the airport building I tried to put a smile on my face. But it was difficult to keep it there as I tried, without luck, to find my group.

'Wild Country, Walking in Provence?' I asked any group of more than four people, but they all looked at me as if I was mad. I was beginning to think I'd got the wrong time or come to the wrong airport when I saw *him* — Grant Cooper. My heart immediately gave a jump, and not just because I was nervous about being late. I didn't like Grant, but he was very good-looking. I'd liked the look of him when I first met him. But then I'd spoken to him, and all that changed.

I just didn't find him easy to get on with. Every time he spoke to me I felt he was laughing at me. It made me so mad I wanted to scream.

As I got closer, I could see that Grant had already found the group. There was nothing else to do but walk up to them with a big Wild Country smile on my face.

'Hello, everybody,' I said. 'I'm Tess Marriot, one of your tour leaders. I hope you had a good journey?'

'Hello, Tess,' Grant said. 'Did you get lost on your way to the airport?'

3 [SPEAKING] Work in pairs. Discuss these questions.

1 Imagine you're Tess. What's your answer to Grant's question at the end of the extract?

2 In the extract we learn that 'doing a Tess Marriot' means making a mistake.

 a Think of a famous person who is well known for certain actions or qualities. How could that person's name be used?

> I think 'doing a Beyoncé' could mean singing really well and dancing at the same time.

 b How would you like *your* name to be used?

WRITING
A reply to a letter asking for advice

1 Read the letter and the reply. Answer the questions.

1 What is Alan's problem?
2 What question does Susannah suggest that Alan asks himself?

2 Complete the missing words from Susannah's reply.

1 This is the first question you _____ _____ ask yourself.
2 If the answer is no, then maybe _____ _____ end the friendship now.
3 … you _____ _____ talk to him about the name-calling …
4 … and explain that he _____ _____ stop saying those things.
5 Finally, _____ _____ _____ _____ to talk to your parents.

3 Read Susannah's reply again. In which paragraph does she …

1 offer advice to make the friendship work?
2 outline Alan's problem?
3 tell him to speak to others about his problem?
4 ask Alan to think more carefully about the situation?

4 Read another letter to Susannah. Write three pieces of advice for Lara.

5 Write a reply to Lara (150–200 words). Say what you think she should do.

Susannah's advice page

Write with your problem and Susannah will give you advice. This week's letter is from Alan in Salisbury, UK.

Dear Susannah,

Last month, we moved to a new town. My parents quickly made friends with the people who live next door. They've got a son of about my age. He's friendly and invites me to do things with him. But the thing is, when we see other kids, he calls them names and makes horrible comments. He wants me to join in, but I don't want to.

What can I do? If I tell my parents, it'll be hard because they really like his parents. And to be honest, I haven't got many other friends yet. If I stop hanging out with him, maybe he'll start calling me names too.

What should I do?

Alan, Salisbury

Dear Alan,

It's often difficult to make new friends when you move town, so it was almost perfect that your new neighbours had a son your age and that he wanted to be your friend. What a shame that you're finding it difficult to spend time with him.

You don't say in your letter if you think you could be friends if his behaviour was better. This is the first question you ought to ask yourself. If the answer is no, then maybe you'd better end the friendship now. Don't worry – I'm sure you'll soon make lots of friends when you start school.

However, if you think you could be friends, then you should definitely talk to him about the name-calling and explain that he had better stop saying those things. If he's going to be a good friend, he'll listen to you. If he ignores you, then this friendship probably isn't going to work.

Finally, it's a good idea to talk to your parents. They're the people who know you best and are often the best people to give you advice.

Good luck!

Susannah

Dear Susannah,

I have very bad eyesight and need to wear glasses. Because of this, some people at school call me names. I tried not to let it bother me too much, but the problem is that it happens quite often. I've always enjoyed school and had lots of friends, but I'm starting to hate going there. My grades are also getting worse and some of the teachers have said they're disappointed with me. I know I should talk to the teachers, but I'm sure this is only going to make things worse. Can you help?

Lara, Ipswich

4 DILEMMAS

OBJECTIVES

FUNCTIONS: talking about hypothetical situations; expressing wishes; apologising and accepting apologies

GRAMMAR: first and second conditional (review); time conjunctions; *wish* and *if only*; third conditional (review)

VOCABULARY: being honest; making a decision; *now*

READING

1 Read the definition. Then look at the pictures. What dilemmas do you think they show?

> **dilemma:** a situation in which a difficult choice has to be made between two or more alternatives

2 Read the quiz quickly. Match each picture with a question.

3 ◀))1.25 Read the quiz again and listen. Then complete it with your answers. Compare with a partner.

4 Match these responses with the quiz questions.

☐ **a** I'd try and fix it before she noticed.

☐ **b** I'd keep quiet but make sure I worked really hard for my next test.

☐ **c** I'd ask if I could change it for another one.

☐ **d** I'd write my own answer but then look at her paper to check it.

☐ **e** I'd ask him or her what it was about.

☐ **f** I'd admit I didn't have enough money and ask to borrow some from a friend.

☐ **g** I'd have an argument with them about it.

☐ **h** I'd spend some of it and give some to charity.

What would YOU do?

What would you do if ...

1 you heard a text message arrive on your girlfriend's or boyfriend's phone when he or she was out of the room?

A I wouldn't open it.

B I'd read it and pretend I hadn't.

2 you found €100 in a cash machine outside a bank?

A I'd go into the bank and give it to someone who worked there.

B I'd keep it and buy myself something nice.

3 you noticed your teacher had made a mistake marking your test and given you a better mark?

A I'd tell my teacher about the mistake immediately.

B I wouldn't say anything.

4 you broke your mum's vase while playing football in the house?

A I'd own up and say it was me.

B I'd say that the cat did it.

5 you bought a shirt, wore it to a party once and decided you didn't really like it?

A I'd give it to a friend.

B I'd take it back to the shop, say I'd never worn it and get my money back.

6 there was a party you really wanted to go to, but you thought your parents might not let you go?

A I'd be open, tell them why I wanted to go and accept their decision.

B I'd say I was staying at a friend's house, go to the party and hide the truth from them.

7 you were stuck in a difficult Maths test and noticed that you could easily copy from your friend's paper?

A I wouldn't look. I'd just try harder to answer the question myself.

B I'd look at her paper.

8 you didn't have enough money for a full-price cinema ticket?

A I'd leave and go home.

B I'd lie about my age and try and get in for a cheaper price.

RESULTS

MORE 'A'S THAN 'B'S: You're basically an honest person. You understand that if you always tell the truth, people will trust you. **MORE 'B'S THAN 'A'S:** Sometimes you take the easy way out. Be careful because it may cause you problems. You don't want people to think of you as dishonest.

▮TRAIN TO THiNK ▮

Thinking of consequences

In order to make a good decision, it's important to think of all possible consequences for others and for yourself.

5 Choose four of the questions in the quiz. Think of possible consequences for each option.

Question	Action	Consequence
1	I read the text message.	My girlfriend / boyfriend gets angry and doesn't trust me any more. We stop being friends.
	I don't read the text message.	I don't find out what the message is about.

SPEAKING

Work in pairs. Discuss these questions.

1 Which of the situations in the quiz is the most / least serious?

2 Do you agree with what the results say about you?

GRAMMAR
First and second conditional (review)

1 Complete these sentences from the quiz on page 39 with the correct forms of the verbs. Then match them with the parts of the rule.

1 What _____ you _____ (do) if you _____ (break) your mum's vase while playing football?

2 If you always _____ (tell) the truth, people _____ (trust) you.

> **RULE:**
> - We use the **first conditional** to talk about real situations and their consequences. We form it with *if* + present simple / future (*will*) clause. _____
> - We use the **second conditional** to talk about hypothetical or very unlikely situations and their outcomes. We form it with *if* + past simple / *would* clause. _____

2 Complete the conditional sentences with the correct forms of the verbs. Think carefully about whether each one is a first or second conditional.

What should I do?

Why is Jan so mean to me? If Jan [1] _____ (not be) so mean to me, I [2] _____ (want) to invite her to my party. The problem is, she's so popular. If she [3] _____ (not have) so many friends, nobody [4] _____ (care) if she was at my party or not. I have to invite her. If I [5] _____ (not invite) Jan to my party, nobody [6] _____ (come) to it.

Maybe I shouldn't have a party. But if I [7] _____ (not have) a party, I [8] _____ (not get) any presents and I want presents! Why are birthdays always so much trouble? If it [9] _____ (not be) my birthday next week, my life [10] _____ (not be) so complicated. If I [11] _____ (know) what to do, I [12] _____ (do) it. But I don't!

Workbook page 36

Time conjunctions

3 Complete the sentences with the words.

unless | if | until | when | as soon as

1 I don't know where he is, but I'll tell him _____ I see him.

2 I'm meeting him later, so I'll tell him _____ I see him.

3 It's really important. I'm going to tell him _____ I see him.

4 I won't tell him anything _____ he asks.

5 I'll work _____ he arrives and then I'll stop.

4 Complete the sentences so that they are true for you. Tell your partner.

1 As soon as I get home tonight, I …

2 If the weather is good this weekend, I …

3 When I'm 18, I …

4 Unless I get lots of homework this weekend, I …

5 I'm going to save all my money until …

Workbook page 36

VOCABULARY
Being honest

1 Write the words in the correct columns.

cheat | get away with something
hide the truth | do the right thing
tell a lie | be open about something
tell the truth | own up to something

Positive behaviour	Negative behaviour
	cheat

2 Compete the conversation with the correct form of the verbs from Exercise 1.

DAN I've got a dilemma. The other day I [1] _____ in a test. I copied from Ben.

ANA Why?

DAN Well, I thought I could [2] _____ away with it, but now the teacher wants to know who copied who.

ANA You should [3] _____ up to it and say it was you.

DAN I know, but it's too difficult to [4] _____ the truth.

ANA But you can't [5] _____ the truth now! What about poor Ben? What were you thinking?

DAN It's Maths. I just find it so difficult.

ANA Well, you need to be [6] _____ about this. First, say sorry for cheating and explain why you [7] _____ a lie. Then tell your teacher what the problem is.

DAN You're right, of course. It's just so difficult to [8] _____ the right thing sometimes.

Workbook page 38

LISTENING

1 SPEAKING Work in pairs. Look at the photos. What do you know about these people and characters? What difficulties might they face?

2 🔊 1.26 Listen to the conversation. What are the teenagers doing?

3 🔊 1.26 Listen again. Circle the correct answers.

1 Where are the teenagers?
    A on a long train journey
    B on the platform, waiting for a train
    C at home

2 What do they decide to play?
    A a card game invented by Maddy
    B a guessing game invented by Liam
    C a traditional children's game

3 Why isn't Andy Murray a good choice for this game?
    A Maddy and Susie don't like tennis.
    B He isn't famous enough.
    C He isn't a fictional character.

4 Why does Liam get angry when Maddy guesses Superman?
    A He chose someone too easy.
    B She doesn't let him finish.
    C She got the wrong answer.

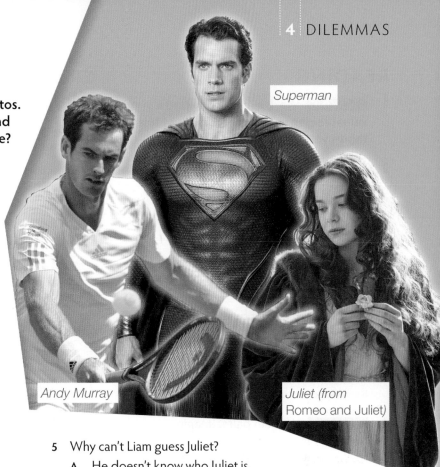

Superman

Andy Murray

Juliet (from Romeo and Juliet)

5 Why can't Liam guess Juliet?
    A He doesn't know who Juliet is.
    B He doesn't know very much about history.
    C He gets angry with Maddy.

6 Why doesn't Maddy say 'Harry Potter' straight away?
    A She's enjoying annoying Liam.
    B She doesn't know who it is.
    C She's bored with the game.

GRAMMAR
wish and *if only*

1 **Read the sentences. Which fictional characters might say them? Complete the rule. Use the sentences to help you.**

1 'I wish I **could** kill Lord Voldemort.'
2 'If only our families **wouldn't** fight all the time.'
3 'I wish Lois Lane **knew** who I really was.'

> **RULE:**
> * We use *wish / if only* + the ¹_____ tense to express how we would like our current situation to be different.
> * We use *wish / if only* + ²_____ to say that we'd like the ability or permission to do something.
> * We use *wish / if only* + ³_____ to complain about a situation that we don't like.

> **LOOK!** We can use *was* or *were* after a singular subject (*I, he, she* or *it*) when we express wishes.
> *I wish I **was** older. / I wish I **were** older.*

2 **Complete the sentences with the correct forms of the verbs.**

see | stop | not get
not be | not fight | have

1 I wish this train journey _____ so long.
2 I wish Liam _____ talking for a while.
3 If only I _____ an interesting book with me.
4 I wish Maddy _____ with me all the time.
5 If only Maddy _____ so angry with me.
6 I wish Maddy _____ that I'm in love with her!

3 SPEAKING Play 'famous wishes' in groups of four.

* Choose a famous fictional person and write three wishes. (Remember: they should be about the present situation, not the past.)
* Read out your sentences. The other students have to guess who you are.

Workbook page 37 ➡

READING

1 **SPEAKING** Work in pairs. You find a valuable ring in the street. Think of four things you could do with it.

2 Read the story. What did Billy do with the ring?

3 Read the story again. Who do you think said these things?

 1 'If only a little good luck came my way.'
 2 'What's that in my cup?'
 3 'I'd like to buy it.'
 4 'It's a lot of money, but I can't.'
 5 'I was here a few days ago.'
 6 'I can't believe he didn't sell my ring!'
 7 'I think that's a great idea.'
 8 'We never thought we'd see you again.'

4 **SPEAKING** Work in pairs. Imagine this story is going to be made into a Hollywood film. Discuss these questions.

 1 Which actors are you going to choose to play the main characters?
 2 How are you going to give the film a big 'Hollywood ending'?
 3 What's the title of your film?

5 Share your ideas with the class.

GRAMMAR
Third conditional (review)

1 Complete these sentences from the story with the correct forms of the verbs. Then complete the rule.

 1 If Billy _____ (look) up, he _____ (see) a young lady on her way to work.
 2 If he _____ (not do) the right thing, he _____ (not see) his sisters again.

> **RULE:** We use the **third conditional** to talk about situations and their outcomes in the past. We form it with:
> *if* + [1] _____ + *would(n't) have* + [2] _____ .

2 Complete the third conditional sentences.

 0 If Billy *had been* on a different street, Sarah *wouldn't have seen* him.
 1 Sarah _____ (see) the ring if she _____ (look) in the cup.
 2 Billy _____ (keep) the ring if Sarah _____ (not return).
 3 Sarah _____ (not raise) so much money if she _____ (not put) her story on the Internet.

3 Complete the sentences so that they are true for you.

 1 If I hadn't gone to school today, …
 2 I'd have been really happy if …
 3 If I'd been born 100 years ago, …

Workbook page 37

The day Billy Ray's life changed forever

Billy Ray Harris was homeless. He spent each day on the streets of Kansas City, begging for money for food and maybe a bed for the night. Every day, as he sat thinking about his life, he occasionally heard the sound of a coin or two dropping into his cup. One day, the noise was louder than usual. If Billy had looked up, he'd have seen a young lady on her way to work. But he didn't. A little later, when he looked into the cup, he could hardly believe what he saw. At the bottom was a shining diamond ring.

Billy's first thought was to go straight to a jeweller's and that's exactly what he did. To his complete amazement, he was offered $4,000. Billy thought long and hard. Was this a mistake? It was more money than he'd seen in a long time. But then he thought about his grandfather, who had brought him up always to do the right thing, and knew he had to reconsider. His mind was made up. He'd keep the ring and maybe one day its owner would return.

In fact, he didn't have to wait long. Two days later, a young woman approached him while he was begging. She introduced herself as Sarah Darling and asked if he'd found anything unusual in his cup. Billy reached into his pocket and pulled out the ring. When he saw the smile on Sarah's face he knew he'd made the right decision. She explained that when she dropped the coins into his cup, she'd forgotten putting her ring in her purse.

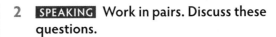

VOCABULARY
Making a decision

1 Match 1–8 with the <u>underlined</u> words and phrases in the text below.

1 for a long time   5 make
2 a good   6 thought again about
3 the wrong   7 original idea
4 decide   8 made a new decision

My ᵃ<u>first thought</u> was to go with the blue. But then I thought ᵇ<u>long and hard</u> and ᶜ<u>changed my mind</u>. Maybe the red was better. But had I made ᵈ<u>the right</u> decision? Had I? I ᵉ<u>reconsidered</u> my choice. Red or blue? Red or blue? Why was it so difficult to ᶠ<u>make up my mind</u>? Well, I didn't want to make ᵍ<u>a bad</u> decision, did I? So I called my sister. Maybe she could help me ʰ<u>come to</u> a decision.
'Yes, what is it?' she asked.
'Red or blue?' I asked.
'I don't know why you're asking me,' she said. 'You only ever wear blue.'

But the story doesn't end there. Sarah told her husband the story and how she wanted to post it on the Internet. He thought it was a good idea. They also set up an online appeal to raise money for Billy. They soon had more than $185,000.

Billy Ray Harris no longer spends his days begging. He has a home and a job. The story also made the local news and he was reunited with his two sisters, who he hadn't seen for over 16 years. If he hadn't done the right thing, he wouldn't have seen his sisters again.

Sedalia

2 **SPEAKING** Work in pairs. Discuss these questions.

1 What's the biggest decision you've ever made?
2 Have you ever made the wrong decision? What was it?
3 How good are you at making your mind up about small things?
4 What sort of things do you usually need to think long and hard about?
5 Do you ever reconsider decisions you have made?
6 Who do you ask to help you come to important decisions?

Workbook page 38

THiNK VALUES
Doing the right thing

1 Think about a time when you had to make a difficult decision. Make notes.

1 What decision did you make?
2 What were the consequences?

2 Write a short paragraph. Include a third conditional sentence.

Last year, there was a new student in my class. Nobody wanted to sit next to him, so I did. I'm really happy I did. If I hadn't sat next to him, he wouldn't have become my best friend. What a good decision I made!

3 Read your paragraph out to the class. Then vote on the best story.

WRITING
A diary entry about a dilemma

Choose one of these situations or use your own idea. Write a diary entry about it (150–200 words). Try to use language from this unit.

1 Explain the problem.
2 Think about two possible solutions and their consequences.
3 Decide what you're going to do and why.

- You've got a detention. If you tell your parents, you won't be allowed to go to a party.
- It's your mum's birthday this weekend, but you spent all your money on clothes and haven't got any left to buy her a present.
- You saw your best friend's boyfriend / girlfriend at the cinema with another boy / girl.

And the hole gets deeper!

1 **Look at the photos and answer the questions.**

What is Jeff holding?
Who seems very interested in Mia's friend?

2 🔊 1.27 **Now read and listen to the photostory. Check your answers.**

1

FLORA What's with the helmet, Jeff?

JEFF It's my dad's. He does go-karting.

MIA Oh yeah, I remember now. You told us about that. He's pretty good, isn't he?

JEFF Oh yeah, he's really into it. He goes all the time now that he's got his own go-kart. Anyway, there's a problem with his helmet, so he asked me to take it to the shop.

MIA Oh, look! There's Chloë.

LEO Who's that?

MIA She's a friend of mine, from when I used to be in the orchestra.

JEFF Wow, she's pretty! If I'd known she was in the orchestra, I would have come to more concerts!

2

CHLOE Hi, Mia. What a nice surprise! How are you?

MIA Good, thanks, Chloë. These are my friends, Leo, Jeff and Flora.

CHLOE Hi, nice to meet you all. Hey, is that a motorbike helmet?

JEFF Well, actually, it's a go-kart helmet. It's …

CHLOE So, you're a go-karter? Cool! I've always wanted to try go-karting!

JEFF Well, um, yes. It's just a hobby. But I race too, you know, now and again. Believe it or not, I've even won a few times.

CHLOE Wow! You actually race. That's so cool. I'd really like to try go-karting, but I've never had the chance.

JEFF Oh, that's a shame. It's good fun.

CHLOE I'm sure it is. Do you think I could … ?

JEFF What?

CHLOE Well, I was wondering if I could come along with you sometime, maybe watch you race. Any chance?

JEFF Oh, um, well, maybe. I mean, yes, of course. That would be great.

CHLOE Cool! So, when's your next race?

JEFF Um … Let me think. I'm not sure, to be honest.

CHLOE Well, look, when you know, call me, OK? Mia's got my number.

3

CHLOE Talk to you soon, I hope, Jeff. Bye, everyone!

JEFF Yeah, see you, Chloë.

FLORA Are you out of your mind? You aren't a go-karter, and just now you said you were. Why did you do that?

MIA Do you need to ask?

JEFF Well, she seemed really nice, you know, and she likes go-karting.

LEO Between you and me, I think Jeff has just dug himself into a big hole.

MIA Yes, I think you might be right. What are you going to do now, Jeff?

DEVELOPING SPEAKING

3 Work in pairs. Discuss what happens next in the story. Write down your ideas.

We think Jeff asks his dad to help him.

4 ▶ **EP2** Watch and find out how the story continues.

5 Mark the sentences T (true) or F (false).

1 Jeff phones Chloë. ☐
2 Chloë asks Jeff if he's really a go-karter. ☐
3 Jeff goes to the go-kart track with his father. ☐
4 Jeff makes a film of himself driving a go-kart. ☐
5 Jeff and Chloë arrange to meet on Sunday. ☐
6 Jeff pretends that he's hurt his knee. ☐
7 His trick is discovered when he uses his phone. ☐
8 Chloë never wants to see Jeff again. ☐

PHRASES FOR FLUENCY

1 Find these expressions in the photostory. Who says them? How do you say them in your language?

1 What's with (the helmet)?
2 Believe it or not, …
3 I was wondering if …
4 Any chance?
5 Are you out of your mind?
6 Between you and me, …

2 Use the expressions in Exercise 1 to complete the conversations.

1 A Andy, _____ you could take Billy for a walk.
  B Sorry, I can't. _____ , I'm really scared of dogs.
2 A Hi, Steve. Wow! _____ those really old football boots?
  B They're ancient, aren't they? _____ , my dad used to wear them when he was at school. I need new ones.
3 A Hi, Jane. My phone's broken. I need to use yours. _____ ?
  B _____ ? It's brand new! I wouldn't lend it to anyone!

Pronunciation
Consonant–vowel word linking
Go to page 120. 🔊

WordWise

now

1 Look at the words and phrases in bold in these sentences from the photostory. Match them with the definitions.

1 Oh yeah, I remember **now**.
2 He goes all the time **now that** he's got his own go-kart.
3 But I race too, you know, **now and again**.
4 You aren't a go-karter, and **just now** you said you were.
5 What are you going to do **now**, Jeff?

a in the near future
b at this moment
c a moment or two ago
d because finally
e sometimes

2 Use words and phrases from Exercise 1 to complete the sentences.

1 I've finished my work, so _____ I'm going to hang out with my friends.
2 I don't listen to this music all the time, but _____ I like to play it.
3 Sally was here _____ , but she's gone out.
4 I'll eat later. I'm not hungry _____ .
5 I don't walk to school _____ I've got a bike.

Workbook page 38 ▶

FUNCTIONS
Apologising and accepting apologies

1 Write the expressions in the correct columns.

No problem. | I'm so sorry. | I feel awful about this.
That's / It's OK. | I don't know what to say.
Don't worry about it. | No worries | I'm so ashamed.

Apologising	Accepting apologies

2 Work in pairs. Imagine you're in these situations and act out conversations. Use expressions from Exercise 1.

● A has spilled a drink on B's trousers.
● A has arrived very late for a meeting with B.
● A has bumped into B and B has fallen over.
● A has completely forgotten B's name.

LISTENING
Part 1: Multiple choice

Workbook page 35

1 🔊 1.30 **You will hear people talking in eight different situations. For questions 1–8, choose the best answer (A, B or C).**

   1 You hear a boy talking about how he got his name. Why was it hard for his parents to name him?
      A   They each wanted different names.
      B   There weren't many possibilities for a name that worked in two languages.
      C   He was born two weeks early.

   2 You hear a girl talking on her phone. What is her problem?
      A   She doesn't want to invite Lucy to her birthday celebration.
      B   Her mum said that Lucy can't come for a sleepover.
      C   She really wants to have a big party.

   3 You hear part of an interview with a footballer. What does he find most difficult about his job?
      A   not being free at weekends
      B   having to work out every day
      C   the comments some of the fans make

   4 You hear two friends talking about a camping trip. What advice does Alan give Steve?
      A   to take a comfortable sleeping bag
      B   to get a lift to the campsite
      C   not to take things that weigh too much

   5 You hear a local news report. What did Clive Roberts think when he found the money?
      A   I'm £10,000 richer.
      B   How can I return this to the owner?
      C   Could I keep this? Would anybody ever know?

   6 Two friends are talking about a party. Why did Chloë miss the party?
      A   Her dad said she had to go cycling with him.
      B   She fell asleep in the middle of the day.
      C   She was watching TV and forgot the time.

   7 You hear a girl talking about a difficult decision. Why did she find it hard to choose which exams to take?
      A   She had no idea about what career she wanted to do.
      B   She didn't want to disappoint her dad.
      C   She wanted to make sure her exams would help her get a well-paid job.

   8 You hear a book review on the radio. What did Carla like best about the book?
      A   that she was able to understand the story
      B   that it was a love story
      C   the way the characters developed during the story

WRITING
Part 2: Story

Workbook page 43

2 **Your English teacher has asked you to write a short story for the school's new website. The story must begin or end with the following words:**

That name! Why did my parents give me that stupid name?!

Write your story in 140–190 words.

TEST YOURSELF

VOCABULARY

1 **Complete the sentences with the words / phrases in the list. There are four extra words / phrases.**

brand | call | chain | cheat | consumers | get away with | image
logo | manufacturer | make | name | own up to | products | tell

1 She worked very hard for years before she started to _____ a name for herself in the theatre.
2 The company was in trouble until they started making some new _____ .
3 If you _____ during the exam, we'll take you out of the exam room and destroy your paper.
4 I like so many different kinds of music. Basically, you _____ it, I like it!
5 He tried to look at another boy's test, but the teacher saw him so he didn't _____ it.
6 I think it's so childish when you _____ other people names.
7 We didn't like our old _____ so we got a new one designed. It's on our website now.
8 Did you eat the last piece of apple pie? Come on – _____ me the truth!
9 We started with just one shop, but now we have a _____ of twenty.
10 I know you took my things without asking. Why don't you just _____ it?

/10

GRAMMAR

2 **Complete the sentences with the words in the list. There are two extra words.**

better | if | go | ought | unless | until | went | when

1 It's pretty late – I think I have to _____ now, OK?
2 I really wish we _____ out to eat more often.
3 I'll call you _____ the film finishes, OK?
4 I'm not going to bed _____ I finish this book – it's brilliant!
5 You'll never be his friend _____ you go and talk to him!
6 It's a secret, so you'd _____ not tell anyone else!

3 **Find and correct the mistake in each sentence.**

1 You shouldn't to talk to me like that. It isn't nice.
2 If they wouldn't be so expensive, I'd buy some of those chocolates.
3 I wish you don't live so far away.
4 Your eye looks bad – I think you better go to the doctor.
5 If it hadn't rained, we had gone to the beach yesterday.
6 If only we can see you more often.

/12

FUNCTIONAL LANGUAGE

4 **Circle the correct words.**

1 A I think we *should / ought* to go now.
  B That's a shame. If only you *could stay / stayed* a little longer.
2 A Listen, *we mustn't / we don't have to* miss the train tomorrow morning.
  B You're right. *I'd better not / I don't have to* forget to set the alarm on my phone.
3 A Hey! Stop! You *don't / can't* come in here. You're too young!
  B Sorry! But I really want to see the film. I wish I *would be / were* eighteen already!

/8

4 A Patrick *wouldn't have / won't have* come to the party if he'd known Sue was going to be there.
  B Yeah, it's a shame – if only *we'd told / we've told* him earlier.

MY SCORE [ ] /30

| 22 – 30 |
| 10 – 21 |
| 0 – 9 |

47

5 WHAT A STORY!

OBJECTIVES

FUNCTIONS: telling a story
GRAMMAR: relative pronouns; defining and non-defining relative clauses; relative clauses with *which*
VOCABULARY: types of story; elements of a story

READING

1 **Think of an example of each of these things.**

- a story or a favourite fairy tale from your childhood
- a favourite film
- a thriller (either a book or a film) that really grabbed you
- an anecdote or a joke you've heard recently

2 SPEAKING **Work in pairs. Share one or two of your ideas from Exercise 1.**

3 SPEAKING **Why do you think people like stories so much? With a partner, discuss as many reasons as you can think of. Then compare your ideas with the rest of the class.**

4 🔊 1.31 **Read and listen to the article. Were your ideas the same as the writer's?**

5 **Read the article again. Answer the questions using evidence from the text.**

1 What examples does the writer give to show that storytelling is popular in the modern world?
2 What point is the writer making in paragraph 2?
3 What did the Neanderthal man *not* want to do when telling the story?
4 How have storytellers contributed to society in different cultures?
5 How did storytellers manage to keep people interested in their stories over the years?
6 Why can stories be very important for a country and its culture?

■ TRAIN TO THiNK ■

Thinking about different writing styles

Writers use different techniques to bring their texts alive.

6 **Answer the questions.**

1 What technique does the writer use in the title of the article?
2 How many times does he use this technique in the article?
3 Why do you think he does this?

7 **Choose the correct option.**

1 When people ask a rhetorical question, they …
   A expect an answer.
   B don't really expect an answer.
2 They ask a rhetorical question to …
   A introduce a subject they want to talk about.
   B find out what you're thinking.

8 **Paragraphs 4 and 5 don't contain any rhetorical questions. Think of a rhetorical question that you could add to each paragraph.**

Everybody loves stories – but why?

What's the first image that comes to mind when you hear the word 'storytelling'? A parent who's reading a fairy tale to their little child – that's what most of us think of immediately. But there's more to stories, of course. What about our favourite movies, the thriller we're reading right now, and that friend who's so brilliant at telling jokes and anecdotes that everyone loves listening to? The movies, the thrillers, the anecdotes and the jokes: they all have something in common with fairy tales. They're all based on the same activity, which is one of the most exciting things humans can do: telling stories!

But why do we tell stories? Just for fun? Well, here's a story for you. Imagine the world hundreds of thousands of years ago. A group of Neanderthals are sitting around the fire in a cave, where they've just finished eating a big meal together. One of them has an idea. He wants to get some berries, which he wants to share with everybody.

His friend decides to join him. Off they go, out of the cave, down to the place where the best berries grow. Well, they don't come back for a long while, and finally, the only one of them to return is the friend, who's covered in blood and has a sad story to share. He tells the others that as soon as they went round the bend, not far from the cave, a sabre-toothed tiger attacked them and killed his friend. The others are shocked, of course, but they're also warned.

Are you getting the idea? Stories aren't just about entertainment. Good stories engage us emotionally, and they do that by giving us something to think about. They contain messages which might be useful for us in the future, like the Neanderthal man's story, which certainly wasn't intended to entertain his friends!

We admire people whose magical storytelling skills capture our attention and our imagination. Everybody has always respected storytellers, who have been important members of many societies. In the past, storytellers often travelled a lot. When they went to places far away, their stories travelled with them. When they returned home, they had new stories to share. People were eager to listen, which was fun but also gave them a chance to learn about those remote places.

In cultures all over the world, important stories have been passed down from generation to generation. These stories come from previous generations, whose wisdom and knowledge they contain. They're often about disasters, dramatic events such as fires, storms, thunder, lightning and floods. Every country and culture has its own stories. Our stories have become part of our tradition. Our stories reflect who we are.

SPEAKING

Work in pairs. Discuss these questions.

1   What kind of stories do you enjoy most? Give an example.
2   Have you ever told someone a story that your parents or grandparents told you? Where did they hear the story?

GRAMMAR
Relative pronouns

1 **Complete these sentences from the article on page 49. Then complete the rule.**

1 A group of Neanderthals are sitting around the fire in a cave, _____ they've just finished eating a big meal together.

2 He wants to get some berries, _____ he wants to share with everybody.

3 Everybody has always respected storytellers, _____ have been important members of many societies.

4 These stories come from previous generations, _____ wisdom and knowledge they contain.

> **RULE:** We use relative clauses to give extra information. We use …
> 1 _____ to refer to **people**.
> 2 _____ to refer to **things**.
> 3 _____ to refer to **possessions**.
> 4 _____ to refer to **places**.

2 **Combine the sentences by replacing the <u>underlined</u> words with relative pronouns from Exercise 1.**

1 One of the world's greatest storytellers is Stephen King. <u>He</u> has sold more than 400 million books.

2 Many people love his horror stories. <u>The horror stories</u> are often quite shocking.

3 The best storyteller I know is my uncle. <u>He</u> lived in India for several years.

4 We love listening to our English teacher. <u>Her</u> stories are fascinating.

5 At our school we have a great library. We like to relax and read <u>there</u>.

Workbook page 46

Defining and non-defining relative clauses

3 **Complete these sentences from the article on page 49. Then read the rule.**

1 What's the first image _____ comes to mind when you hear the word 'storytelling'?

2 A parent _____'s reading a fairy tale to a little child – that's what most of us think of immediately.

3 Off they go, out of the cave, down to the place _____ the best berries grow.

4 The only one of them to return is the friend, _____'s covered in blood.

5 We admire people _____ magical storytelling skills capture our attention and our imagination.

> **RULE:** We use a **defining relative clause** to identify an object, a person, a place or a possession. Without this information, it's hard to know who or what we're talking about.
> *The man was angry. (Which man?)*
> *The man **whose bag had been stolen** was angry.*
> We use a **non-defining relative clause** to add extra information. We don't need this information to understand the sentence. We put commas around it.
> *Stephen King is a famous writer.*
> *Stephen King, **who is American**, is a famous writer.*
> (Extra information: he's American.)

4 **Complete these defining relative clauses with *who*, *where*, *whose* or *that*.**

1 The house _____ I grew up is next to a school.

2 A book _____ has lots of short chapters is perfect for the bus ride to school.

3 A person _____ knows a lot of jokes is usually a good public speaker.

4 We went to hear a lecture by a writer _____ books are always on the best-seller list.

5 The author _____ wrote the famous teen novel *The Outsiders* was only sixteen.

5 **Tick (✓) the sentences which contain non-defining relative clauses and add commas.**

1 My brother is someone who just doesn't like listening to jokes. ☐

2 Fairy tales which were written for children are now being adapted for the cinema. ☐

3 The Brothers Grimm whose stories have fascinated millions of children lived in the 19th century. ☐

4 It's difficult to read in places where people are talking on mobile phones. ☐

Workbook page 46

VOCABULARY
Types of story

1   🔊 1.32 Match the types of story with the book covers. Write numbers 1–9 in the boxes. Then listen and check.

1   crime novel
2   science fiction novel
3   historical novel
4   horror story
5   (auto)biography
6   short stories
7   romantic novel
8   travel literature
9   poetry

Darwin — A ☐
Freddie's War — B ☐
Tales of Terror — C ☐
Love in the L D ☐
THE POETRY OF WAR — E ☐
WAR WORLDS — F ☐
BERLIN EXPRESS — G ☐
The University Murders — H ☐
D·H·LAWRENCE THE VICAR'S GARDEN AND OTHER STORIES — I ☐

2   Which are non-fiction?

3   **SPEAKING** Which types of story do you like reading most? Workbook page 48 ➡

SPEAKING

1   Work in pairs. If you had to choose one of the books in the previous exercise, which would it be and why?

> I'd choose … because the cover looks / the title sounds (exciting / funny / interesting / …).

2   Prepare a one-minute talk about reading. Think about the following points and take notes.

- if you prefer articles, short stories, novels, etc.
- where and when you like reading

3   Take turns giving your talks in small groups.

LISTENING

1   Find out how much your class knows about Stephen King. Then read the biographical data.

Stephen King: fact file

- King was born in 1947 in Portland, Maine.
- He wanted to be a teacher, but couldn't get a job. He worked in a laundry and did various other jobs while continuing to write stories.
- He published his first book, *Carrie*, in 1974. It became a huge success.
- He's written about 50 novels and over 200 horror, fantasy and science fiction short stories. Many of them have become successful films.

2   🔊 1.33 Listen to two teenagers talking about a short story by Stephen King called *Word Processor of the Gods*. What's the last word displayed on the computer screen?

3   🔊 1.33 Listen again and make notes to answer the questions.

1   What has the man always wanted to have? Why?
2   What kind of relationship does he have with his son and his nephew?
3   What event makes the man very unhappy?
4   What happens when he goes to his garden shed the next day?
5   Why does he get angry? What does he do next?
6   What happens at the end?

4   **SPEAKING** Compare your answers in pairs.

▌THiNK SELF-ESTEEM ▌

A better world

SPEAKING Think about these questions. Make notes. Then compare your ideas in class.

1   Imagine you had a machine like the one in the story. If you could eliminate one problem in the world, what would it be? Why?

2   If you could use the machine to create something to make the world a better place, what sentence would you type in?

READING

1 Look at the photos. Do you recognise these fairy tales? Do you know their names in English?

2 Read the article quickly. Who are the Brothers Grimm?

Hollywood fairy tales

Little Red Riding Hood used to be just a story that parents would read to their children at bedtime, but not any more. Now *Red Riding Hood* is a Hollywood blockbuster directed by Catherine Hardwicke. Hardwicke directed *Twilight*, which made her the obvious choice for another film so clearly aimed at the teenage market.

Red Riding Hood isn't the only film to go back to the classic fairy tales and update them for today's teenagers. *Hansel and Gretel: Witch Hunters*, *Jack the Giant Slayer* and *Snow White and the Huntsman* are also hoping they can persuade young people to revisit the stories of their childhood. And then there's *Brothers Grimm*, starring Matt Damon and Heath Ledger, which sees the original authors of many of these fairy tales come face to face with some of their characters. Hollywood, it seems, has realised that fairy tales have the potential to make money, and lots of it.

Teenagers are one of Hollywood's most important markets and after the success of series like *Harry Potter*, *Twilight* and more recently *The Hunger Games*, film studios are looking for more inspiration for stories to keep young people

returning to the cinema. Fairy tales might just be the answer. Many are already quite dark, which makes them ideal for adolescents, who are often fascinated by that side of life. Of course, you might not recognise much of the original story, as extra horror, and romance for the heroes and heroines, have been added to the plots. But with modern-day special effects to bring it all to life, does it really matter?

3 Read the article again and connect the sentences.

1 Catherine Hardwicke has made
2 Several films have been produced
3 *Brothers Grimm* shows how the
4 Films based on fairy tales have
5 Teenagers are often interested
6 When you compare the films to

famous writers meet the heroes
turned out to be extremely
the stories they are based on,
in characters that are evil,
a name for herself as a director
that remind young people of the

stories they enjoyed as children.
you will notice big differences.
of films for a teen audience.
successful commercially.
and villains of their stories.
angry or unhappy.

4 **SPEAKING** Work in pairs. Discuss these questions.

1 What fairy tales are popular in your country?
2 Do you agree that many teenagers are interested in the 'dark' side of life? Why? / Why not?

WRITING
A fairy tale

Think of a fairy tale and write the story (200 words). Think about:

- the ordering of the story.
- how to use a good selection of past tenses.
- how to bring the story alive with adjectives and adverbs.

Don't forget: fairy tales start with *Once upon a time, …* .

GRAMMAR
Relative clauses with *which*

1 Complete these sentences from the article on page 52. Add commas where necessary. What does *which* refer to in each of the sentences? Complete the rule.

1 Hardwicke directed *Twilight* _____ made her the obvious choice for another film so clearly aimed at the teenage market.

2 Many [fairy tales] are already quite dark _____ makes them ideal for adolescents.

> **RULE:** The pronoun [1]_____ normally refers to a noun, but it can sometimes refer to the whole of the previous clause. We cannot use [2]_____ or *that* in the same way.
> *She was late, **which** made her nervous.*
> NOT ~~She was late, **what / that** made her nervous.~~

2 Join the pairs of sentences using *which*.

0 I often play the drums on Sunday mornings. This annoys the neighbours.
I often play *the drums on Sunday mornings, which annoys* the neighbours.

1 She's lost all her money. This means she'll be in trouble.
She's lost _____ in trouble.

2 Nobody in class learned the new words. It was frustrating for our teacher.
Nobody in class _____ for our teacher.

3 Fairy tales have been turned into successful teen films. This has surprised many people.
Fairy tales _____ many people.

4 It's quite amazing that Stephen King manages to write several books per year.
Stephen King _____ quite amazing.

5 It's fascinating that almost all of his books have been made into films.
Almost all of his books _____ fascinating.

3 Complete the sentences so that they are true for you.

0 My favourite singer *is giving a concert in our town next month*, which is fantastic.

1 _____ last year, which made me feel really proud.

2 I heard on the news _____, which I was really upset about.

3 _____, which really isn't easy.

4 SPEAKING Work in pairs. Share your sentences. How long can you keep each conversation going?

> My favourite singer is giving a concert in our town next month, which is fantastic.

> Really? Who's that?

> Lorde.

> Wow! I like her songs too. Do you know when ...?

Workbook page 47

VOCABULARY
Elements of a story

1 Match the words with their definitions.

plot | setting | hero | character
opening | ending | villain | dialogue

1 the story of a film, play, etc.
2 a person in a story
3 the last part of a story
4 the main (usually good) character in a story
5 a character who harms other people
6 the words that the characters say to each other
7 the beginning of a story
8 the time and place in which the action happens

2 Think about these things for two minutes. Make notes.

- a film or book with a great plot
- the setting of the last film you saw
- a film with a great opening
- a good film with a disappointing ending
- an actor who's best at playing villains

3 SPEAKING Work in pairs or small groups. Share your ideas.

Workbook page 48

Culture

1 **Look at the photos and answer the questions.**

1 What can you see in the photos?
2 What do you think the person is doing?
3 Would you like to visit this place? Why (not)?

2 🔊1.34 **Read and listen to the article. Check your answers.**

IRELAND

A nation of storytellers

Hardly any country can claim to have a richer storytelling tradition than Ireland. This is the result of a mixture of many people – the Celts, the Vikings, the Normans and the English – who came to the island at various times and all left a bit of their culture behind.

In the Celtic tradition of spoken storytelling, singers and poets called bards were extremely important people. There was no written language tradition in those days, so bards had to memorise the stories, poems and songs to be able to perform them live. Good storytellers knew hundreds of stories by heart. The stories were the only record of important events, and people appreciated them: they were the best entertainment available.

This tradition has been influential for more than 2,000 years and, in many ways, it's still alive today. Stories have been handed down from generation to generation, with very little change. Storytellers used to move from village to village. Wherever they appeared, they were warmly welcomed, and people gave them food and shelter for the night.

The Irish love of stories can be felt all over the country. In many places, older people still remember the *céilí* (pronounced 'kaylee' and meaning 'get-together'), in which people would meet in a house, sit near the fire, tell stories, sing songs, dance and play music. Interestingly, in recent years, there have been successful attempts to revive this tradition, and some of the most popular contemporary storytellers are very young.

The elegant way talented storytellers use language is called 'the gift of the gab'. If you want to get the gift of the gab, you have to go to Blarney Castle in Cork, in the south of the island. You have to climb to the top of the castle, lie down and bend over backwards to kiss the Stone of Eloquence. And, of course, there's a story to explain this. It tells of an Irish King who rescued a woman when she fell into a river. The woman was so grateful that she cast a spell over him. She gave him the ability to speak so well that he could persuade people to do whatever he wanted. But, for the spell to work, he had to kiss a particular stone on top of Blarney Castle. This is what he did, and it worked. So whoever kisses the Blarney Stone will get the same gift.

You don't believe in such stories? Well, it's true, and you can easily prove it. Just climb to the top of Blarney Castle and kiss that stone …

3 **Read the article again. Mark the sentences T (true) or F (false).**

1 Irish culture has several different influences.
2 Bards used to write down their stories and poems.
3 Irish storytellers were often given hospitality in return for telling stories.
4 It's no longer possible to go to a *céilí*.
5 If people have 'the gift of the gab', they're good at telling stories.

4 **SPEAKING Work in pairs. Discuss these questions.**

1 How does the Irish storytelling tradition compare with storytelling in your country?
2 What stories are there about places near where you live?

5 VOCABULARY There are eight highlighted words or phrases in the text. Match them with these definitions.

1 passed (from older people to younger people)
2 change the position of your body so your head is nearer the floor
3 were able to say from memory
4 bring back to life
5 document
6 said words that had magical powers
7 gave value or importance to
8 a safe place to stay

SPEAKING

1 Look at the pictures. Put them in order and use them to tell a story.

A

B

C

2 🔊 1.37 Listen and compare your story to the one you hear.

Pronunciation

The schwa /ə/ in word endings
Go to page 120. 🔊

FUNCTIONS
Telling a story

1 🔊 1.37 Annie uses these expressions to bring her story to life. Match them with the correct places in the conversation. Then listen again and check.

☐ you'll never believe what
☐ The strangest thing happened to me the other day.
☐ Well, let me finish …
☐ That was the annoying thing.
☐ What are the chances?

ANNIE ¹_____
MAC What?
ANNIE I woke up with this song in my head and I couldn't stop singing it all day long. It was really annoying.
MAC What was it?
ANNIE ²_____ It was a song I knew, but I couldn't remember what it was. I even sang it to a few of my friends, but they didn't know what it was either.
MAC So what was so strange about that?
ANNIE ³_____ I got home from school (with the song still in my head) and I went upstairs to do my homework. I decided to put on the radio to try and forget the song, and ⁴_____ they were playing!
MAC Go on.
ANNIE They were playing the song that I'd been singing all day!
MAC So you'd just been singing a pop song that you'd forgotten the name of.
ANNIE Yes, but the strange thing is that it wasn't a pop song from now. It was some obscure song from the 1980s that you never hear any more. It was a song that my dad used to play when I was really small. I hadn't heard it for years. And they were playing it on the radio! ⁵_____
MAC Yes, that is pretty weird.

2 Think of a strange story that happened to you or to someone else.

- Write down the main events in note form.
- Think how you can use some of the expressions.
- In groups, tell your stories.

HOW DO THEY DO IT?

READING

1 **SPEAKING** Work in pairs. Discuss these questions.

   1 What magicians can you name?
   2 What magic tricks have you seen?
   3 Can you do any tricks yourself? What are they?

2 **Read and listen to the article about Dynamo. Which four of his tricks does it mention?**

3 ◄⑴1.38 **Read the article again and match sentences a–g with spaces 1–6. There's one extra sentence which doesn't belong in the text. Then listen and check.**

   ☐ a He won a few local and national Magic Circle championships.

   ☐ b This wasn't the first time Dynamo had amazed the people of London.

   ☐ c The man was walking on water!

   ☐ d Was he going to throw himself in?

   ☐ e His grandfather was a keen amateur magician and taught Stephen many of his tricks.

   ☐ f Dynamo refuses to tell anyone how he does his tricks.

   ☐ g Was he really walking on air?

■ TRAIN TO THiNK ■

Understanding what's relevant

To write a good text, a writer must make sure that each sentence is linked to what comes before it. Understanding how this is done will help you to do tasks like Exercise 3.

4 **Choose the sentence which *doesn't* have any relevance to the first.**

   Dynamo has a TV series.
   A It's watched by millions of people.
   B Lots of famous guests appear on it.
   C TV is popular with teens all over the world.
   D It's been running for three years now.

5 **Work in pairs. Use this sentence to make a similar task for your partner.**

   Dynamo has amazed the people of London twice.
   A _____   C _____
   B _____   D _____

The man who walks on air

One Saturday afternoon in June, in the busy streets of central London, something strange happened. A man was seen apparently floating beside a London bus as it drove about town. One of his arms was stretched out and was attached to the roof of the bus. This arm appeared to be the only thing supporting the rest of his body. The man waved to the crowds with his other hand and moved his legs. 1_____ How was it possible? It turned out to be the latest illusion from Dynamo, one of the world's most thrilling illusionists and the star of his own TV show, *Dynamo: Magician Impossible*.

2_____ Two years earlier, tourists walking by the River Thames were a little concerned to see a young man go down some steps to the edge of the river and look thoughtfully across to the other side. 3_____ More and more people gathered on the bridge to see what was going on. And then, to their complete disbelief, he lifted up his foot and stepped onto the freezing water. He didn't sink! Then he took another step, and another, and another.

4_____ A few minutes later, when the man was a quarter of the way across the river, a police boat arrived. The man was pulled into the boat and they sped away, leaving a huge crowd of amazed spectators. Of course, hundreds of photos were taken by onlookers and the next day newspapers were full of the fascinating story.

Dynamo is the stage name of Stephen Frayne, who was born in the northern English town of Bradford. 5_____ As a child, Stephen visited New Orleans and saw street magicians for the first time. It was then that Stephen knew he wanted to be a magician when he grew up. He started off learning card tricks and later combined them with a bit of break dancing to create an original act. He was soon making a name for himself.

6_____ A TV show quickly followed, and featured celebrities including Dizzee Rascal, Ms Dynamite, Will Smith and One Direction. As his famous guests watched, Dynamo performed tricks like turning a five-pound note into £20 and turning paper butterflies into real ones. But what everyone wants to know now is: after walking on air and walking on water, what is he going to do next?

So how is it done?

Most people agree that the bus illusion involves a fake arm with a metal pole running through it. This arm is attached to the bus and is used to support Dynamo's body. The walking on water illusion is more difficult to explain. Some people think he walks on glass boards that are put in the water before. Others say he's attached by invisible ropes to camouflaged helicopters that fly high above. What do you think?

SPEAKING

Work in pairs. Discuss these questions.

1 How do you think Dynamo walked on water?
2 Why do you think people enjoy magic tricks so much?

Pronunciation
The /ʒ/ phoneme
Go to page 120.

GRAMMAR
Present and past passive (review)

1 **Complete these sentences from the article on page 57. Use the correct form of *be*. Then complete the rule with *by*, *be* and *past participle*.**

1 The man _____ pulled into the boat …

2 Of course, hundreds of photos _____ taken by onlookers …

3 This arm _____ attached to the bus and _____ used to support Dynamo's body.

4 Some people think he walks on glass boards that _____ put in the water before.

> **RULE:** We form the **passive** with a form of the verb
> ¹_____ and the ²_____ .
> We use the preposition ³_____ to say who or what does the action, but only if this is important.

2 **Complete the instructions with the correct active or passive forms of the verbs.**

use | cut | put over | hold | pull | get | push | hide

0 A long box *is used* for this trick.

1 One woman _____ at one end of the box.

2 A second woman _____ into the box.

3 She puts her head out of one end and _____ her legs to her chest with her arms. At the same time, the first woman _____ her legs out of the other end.

4 The box _____ in half by the magician.

5 The ends of the box _____ apart to show that it has been cut in two.

Workbook page 54 ▶

VOCABULARY
Extreme adjectives and modifiers

1 **Look at these phrases from the article on page 57. What do the adjectives in bold mean?**

1 one of the world's most **thrilling** illusionists

2 a **huge** crowd of amazed spectators

3 stepped onto the **freezing** water

4 newspapers were full of the **fascinating** story

2 **Match the gradable adjectives 1–5 with the extreme adjectives a–e.**

1 good   a hilarious
2 funny   b delighted
3 happy   c huge / enormous
4 big   d tiny / minute
5 small   e great / fantastic / wonderful / brilliant / amazing

> **LOOK!** We use:
> • *very* with gradable adjectives.
> • *absolutely* with extreme adjectives.
> • *really* with gradable and extreme adjectives.

3 **Look at these examples of adjectives with the modifiers *very*, *really* and *absolutely*. Which combinations are correct and which are incorrect? Mark them ✓ or ✗.**

1 really good   ☐
2 really amazing   ☐
3 very funny   ☐
4 very hilarious   ☐
5 absolutely small   ☐
6 absolutely tiny   ☐

4 **Complete the text with adjectives from Exercise 2. Sometimes more than one answer is possible, but don't use each adjective more than once.**

Last night we went to a magic show. It was very good – in fact, it was absolutely ¹_____ . The magician was really ²_____ – we couldn't stop laughing. In one trick, he had two hats: a really small one and an ³_____ one. But from the big hat he pulled out an absolutely ⁴_____ rabbit and from the small hat he pulled out a huge one. It was great fun and I left feeling really ⁵_____ .

Workbook page 56 ▶

LISTENING

1 🔊 1.41 **Listen to two people talking about a tattoo. Which animal does Dave's tattoo show?**

2 🔊 1.41 **Listen again. Tick (✓) the reasons why Kim is so upset about Dave's tattoo.**

1 She knows his parents will be angry. ☐
2 She thinks it looks terrible. ☐
3 She thinks it was too expensive. ☐
4 She thinks his brother will want to get one too. ☐
5 She thinks he's too young to have a tattoo. ☐

3 **Who says these lines: Kim or Dave? What is the context? Complete the table.**

Who?	What?	Why?
Kim	What?! You've … You've …	She's so shocked at Dave's tattoo that she can't speak.
	So do you like it?	
	Whatever. I like it.	
	I'm going to kill you!	

GRAMMAR

have something done

1 <u>Underline</u> **the subject in each sentence. Do we know who is performing the action? Then complete the rule with *us* and *someone*.**

1 I've had a tattoo done.
2 I can have it removed.
3 I'm going to have my hair dyed.

> **RULE:** We often use the structure **have + object + past participle** when we arrange for [1]_____ to do something for [2]_____. In less formal contexts, *get* often replaces *have*.

2 **Complete the sentences. Use *have* + object + past participle.**

Lord Uppity doesn't do anything himself.
1 He never cooks. He _____ his meals _____ by chefs.
2 He and his wife never do any housework. They _____ it _____ by cleaners.
3 He never goes into shops. He _____ everything _____ by his assistant.
4 Neither he nor his wife drives. They _____ their car _____ by an ex-racing driver.
5 They never organise parties. They _____ them _____ by party organisers.
6 They don't look after their children. They _____ them _____ by a nanny.
Life is boring. There's simply nothing to do!

3 **Use the words to write questions.**

~~hair~~ | wedding cake | car | tattoo
teeth | do | repair | make | ~~cut~~ | clean

0 *Where can you have your hair cut*?
At the To Dye For salon.
1 _____? At Derek's Bakery.
2 _____? At Bridge Street Mechanic's.
3 _____? At Body Art.
4 _____? At the Northgate Dental Surgery.

Workbook page 54 ▶

▌THiNK SELF-ESTEEM ▌

Life changes

1 **Match the photos with 1–4.**
1 'My parents won't let me have my hair dyed.'
2 'What a bad idea it was to get a tattoo!'
3 'I'm not allowed to get my ears pierced.'
4 'It'd be cool to have my head shaved, but Dad wouldn't like it.'

2 SPEAKING **Work in pairs. Think of three reasons why the parents of these teenagers are right.**

3 SPEAKING **What are your feelings about these issues? Tell your partner.**

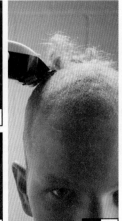

A ☐

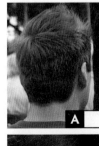

B ☐

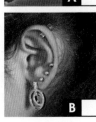

C ☐

D ☐

READING

1 Read the article and number the photos in the order that they are mentioned.

A   B   C   D   E   F

How Do They Do That?

I've just discovered a fantastic new show called *How Do They Do That?* It's one of the best series on TV at the moment! The idea is simple: take a topic – like travel, for example – and then think of lots of little mysteries that could be explained. How do planes take off and land? How do driverless cars work? How do they build model boats in a bottle? That sort of thing. Then get two young, enthusiastic presenters, dress them in white coats and put them in a laboratory to do lots of exciting experiments. Add some cool graphics to explain the rest and there's your show. Get the idea?

Each programme looks at a different subject. As well as *Travel*, topics that have already been covered include *Education*, *The body*, *Around the house* and *Magic* – my favourite so far. Still to come are *Personal finances*, *The natural world*, *Sport* and *Life and how to live it*.

What I like best about the show is that it's fun and you learn something at the same time, so you don't feel so guilty about spending sixty minutes in front of the TV each week. We've been shown how to boil the perfect egg (wash it, put it in boiling water for three minutes and then leave it in the water for a further 60 seconds); how birds make their way back to exactly the same place each summer (they use the stars); and how a touch screen works (that one didn't really make much sense to me). We haven't been shown how to eat chocolate without

putting on weight yet, but I'm still hoping they might include that!

In future programmes, secrets such as how Usain Bolt can run so fast and how spiders make webs will be revealed. The one I'm personally looking forward to the most is how to meet the perfect partner.

So if you aren't already watching *How Do They Do That?*, I strongly recommend that you make time to. It gives you facts that you can use to pretend that you're actually quite intelligent for a while – as long as you can remember them, of course. It's on every Tuesday at 9 pm, but this week's show won't be shown until half an hour later because of the live international football. Get watching and start learning!

2 Read the article again. Answer the questions.

1 What do the presenters wear on *How Do They Do That?* Why do you think they do this?

2 How many different programmes are mentioned?

3 What's the best way to cook an egg?

4 Why couldn't the writer tell you how a touch screen works?

5 What evidence is there that the writer doesn't have a partner?

6 What time will this week's programme start?

3 In which programme are these questions probably answered?

1 How do you buy a house?

2 How do you do well in an exam?

3 How do you do the housework in half an hour?

4 How do whales communicate?

5 How does a GPS work?

4 **SPEAKING** Work in pairs. Choose four of the programmes and think of a question you would like to see answered in each one.

GRAMMAR
Future and present perfect passive (review)

1 Complete the sentences from the article on page 60 with the words in the list. Then complete the rule with *past participle* (x2), *be* and *present perfect*.

been shown | been covered
be shown | be revealed

1 … topics that have already _____ include *Education* …

2 We haven't _____ how to eat chocolate without putting on weight yet …

3 In future programmes, secrets such as how Usain Bolt can run so fast […] will _____ .

4 … but this week's show won't _____ until half an hour later …

> **RULE:**
> * To make the **future passive**, we use *will* + [1]_____ + the [2]_____ .
> * To make the **present perfect passive**, we use the [3]_____ form of *to be* and the [4]_____ .

2 Rewrite the sentences using the passive voice.

1 They will show the match live on TV.

2 They will choose the next Olympic city in April.

3 People all over the world will watch the match.

4 They have already sold all the tickets for the show.

5 They have already made the decision.

6 Someone has already spent that money.

3 Complete the text with the future passive form of the verbs.

Good news for fans of *How Do They Do That?* A new series [1]_____ (film) over the next three months and the new shows [2]_____ (air) in the new year. The shows [3]_____ (present) by Helen, but she [4]_____ (not join) by Liam this time. A new presenter [5]_____ (choose) in the next week – watch this space! The presenters [6]_____ also _____ (join) by Spike the robot dog, but we aren't sure exactly what he'll do. Topics that [7]_____ (cover) include *Buildings*, *Space* and *Food*. There'll also be a new time for the show. It [8]_____ (not show) at the old time of 9 pm on Tuesdays. It [9]_____ (move) to Sunday afternoons at 3 pm and the producers are hoping it [10]_____ (watch) by a bigger audience. I know one person who will be watching for sure – me!

4 Look at the list and write sentences. Use positive and negative present perfect passive forms and *already* or *yet*.

Mum and Dad's anniversary party – things to do

arrange a date for the party ✔
buy decorations ✘
find a place for the party ✔
send invitations ✔
buy drinks ✘
prepare food ✘
hire a DJ ✔
choose music ✘

A date has already been arranged for the party. The decorations haven't been bought yet.

Workbook page 55

VOCABULARY
make and *do*

1 Write the words in the correct columns. Use page 60 to help you.

an experiment | your way | sense
time | money | well | housework

make	do

2 Complete the sentences with the correct form of *make* or *do*.

0 I really need to ___*do*___ well in this test. I'm going to study hard tonight.

1 I've been _____ housework all day. I'm exhausted.

2 It's a really good exhibition. You should _____ time to see it.

3 Sorry I can't meet you at the station, but I'm sure you can _____ your own way to my house.

4 Don't go in there. They're _____ a dangerous experiment.

5 The film is very long, so it _____ sense to have something to eat first.

6 He _____ a lot of money in banking and retired when he was 50.

Workbook page 56

Fiction

friends

sense

make

a cake

time

a noise

1   What is a 'mind map'? What do people use them for?

2   🔊 2.02   **Read and listen to the extract. Answer the questions.**

    1   What is the connection between the mind map and the pendant?

    2   What kind of book do you think *The Mind Map* is?

The Mind Map by David Morrison

*Lucho has always found homework boring. But when he draws
a mind map to plan an essay on stolen gold, something very strange
happens. The mind map is trying to tell him something. But what is it?*

Eva was sitting on the grass with her back to the library, reading her history
textbook. Lucho tried to walk slowly and calmly towards her, but his legs carried him quickly.
Out of the corner of his eye, he could see the little yellow bird flying from one tree to another.

  'Eva,' he said softly.

  Eva turned and looked at him. She was angry.

  'What?' answered Eva. Her voice was cold.

  'You have to believe me, Eva. Something strange is happening. When I was at the computer just now,
the words "Take it back" appeared.'

  'Take what back?' asked Eva. 'What are you talking about?'

  'It's time to show her the pendant,' thought Lucho. His grandmother had told him that one day
the pendant would ask him to take it back home. Eva could help him. He put his hand in his pocket
and brought out the blue bag.

  'Look,' he said. 'I have never shown this to anybody.'

  'What is it?' asked Eva.

  'It's a pendant. I think it might be *guaca*,' he answered.

  Lucho gave the blue bag to Eva. She opened it carefully and took out the pendant.

  'Isn't it beautiful?' asked Lucho.

  'It's very beautiful,' Eva said quietly.

  'My grandmother gave it to me,' he explained. 'She said I had to look after it, but that one day it
would ask me to take it home. I used it to draw the mind map yesterday. I couldn't think what to write in
the circles, so I stopped. When I opened my notebook in the library, I saw those words for the first time.
I'm telling the truth. I promise, Eva.'

  Eva put the pendant back into the blue bag and gave it back to Lucho.

  'My grandmother's name was Esmeralda,' continued Lucho. 'When she was working at the hotel,
an American man gave her the pendant to take care of while he went to Bogotá. The man never returned.
I don't know the name of the hotel but maybe it was the Hotel Continental. I tried to find some
information about it on the Internet, but I couldn't.'

  Eva's phone beeped loudly and they both jumped. She had received a message.

  'What's wrong?' asked Lucho.

  'The message,' she said slowly. 'It says "Take it back".'

  'The same message as the one on the computer screen!' said Lucho slowly. 'Eva, I'm not sure,
but I think the pendant is asking us to help it. I think it's asking us to take it home.'

  'But that's impossible,' said Eva. 'That would be magic.'

  Lucho didn't know what to say. So many strange things had happened since he
had seen the little yellow bird outside the history class window. And now the same
message had appeared on the computer screen and on Eva's phone. Eva was right.
It *was* like magic.

  'Eva,' he said, 'will you help me?'

3 Read the extract again. Mark the sentences T (true) or F (false).

1 This is the first time that Lucho has seen the yellow bird.

2 Eva is upset with Lucho.

3 Lucho's grandmother bought the pendant.

4 Lucho tried to research the Hotel Continental on the Internet.

5 Lucho thinks the pendant is trying to send them a message.

6 The children can't explain how the message got onto Eva's phone.

SPEAKING

Answer the questions in pairs.

1 What do you think is the story behind the pendant?

2 What do you think happens next in the story?

3 What other stories can you think of that involve magical or mysterious objects?

FUNCTIONS
Talking about sequence

Work in pairs. In what order do these things happen when an aeroplane takes off? Discuss your ideas.

First, I think … | After that, … | Next, … | Finally, …

The engine is powered up.

The wheels are pulled up.

The nose is lifted into the air.

The brakes are taken off.

The plane is turned around in the air.

The plane is lined up on the runway.

WRITING
Explaining how things are done

1 Read the explanation and check your answers to the last exercise.

How do planes take off?

To get an aeroplane into the air, you need the correct airspeed. Airspeed is not the speed of the plane, but how fast the air is moving over it. If the plane is facing a strong wind, the airspeed is already quite high. That's why planes are usually lined up to take off facing into the wind.

The engines are turned up to a certain power. Then the brakes are taken off and the plane speeds down the runway. As it does this, air passes over the wings. The wings are curved on the top, so the air has further to travel over the wings than under the wings, and has to travel faster. This creates a force that pushes upwards. When that force is big enough, the nose of the plane is pushed into the air and when the correct airspeed is reached, the whole plane takes off.

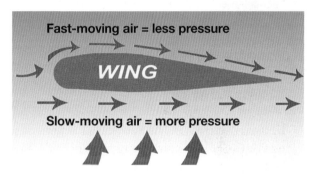
Fast-moving air = less pressure
WING
Slow-moving air = more pressure

When the plane is high enough in the air, the wheels are pulled up and the plane is turned around, leaving space for the next one to take off.

2 Read the explanation again. Use two different-coloured pens to <u>underline</u> …

- the **procedure** (what happens and in what order).
- the **theories** (explanations of why things happen).

3 Choose an activity from the list or your own idea. Write an explanation of how to do it (150 words).

- How to play the guitar
- How to play your favourite computer game
- How to do a headstand

Think about:

- the procedure and the sequence.
- whether you need to explain any theories.
- how to explain any difficult vocabulary.

READING AND USE OF ENGLISH
Part 5: Multiple choice

Workbook page 53 ▶

You are going to read a text about urban legends. For questions 1–4, choose the answer (A, B, C or D) which you think fits best according to the text.

People have been telling stories for as long as they have been walking the Earth. And from cave paintings to Shakespeare's Globe Theatre to Hollywood blockbusters, the methods of telling them have got more and more sophisticated.

In the 1960s, a new storytelling art form emerged – the urban legend. Even if you've never heard the term, you've certainly heard an urban legend. What about the story of the unwanted pet alligators that were flushed down the toilet and are now living in the sewers of New York City? Or the man who woke up in a bathtub full of ice and saw a note informing him that one of his kidneys had been taken out?

One of the key features of the urban legend is its lack of an author. The stories appear mysteriously and are then passed on by word of mouth. And, although we know these mini-tales of horror, humour and embarrassment are almost certainly not true, part of us wants to believe them.

Then the Internet, which is packed with fiction (everything from jokes to the latest releases from top-selling authors), helped create and spread urban legends. Before the Internet, urban legends went around quite slowly. They took time to reach a larger audience. The Internet changed all that almost overnight.

The Internet is the perfect vehicle for the urban legend, for it not only allows the stories to spread much faster but it allows for greater anonymity, too – a lot of what we read online doesn't have an author's name attached to it. This anonymity adds to the overall mystery.

Of course, the Internet also allows you to check the truth of a story more easily. Over time, a number of sites have appeared which collect stories, investigate their origins and report the results. Often there isn't any truth to the story at all. But sometimes the urban legend grew from something that did actually happen. Thanks to the Internet, learning about the origins of an urban legend can be as interesting and entertaining as the story itself.

1 What do we learn about stories from the first paragraph?
   A They've never been as popular as they are now.
   B They have their origins in the days of Shakespeare.
   C They were much longer in the past.
   D Ways of telling them have changed over time.

2 What does the author suggest about urban legends?
   A Everyone knows the term 'urban legend'.
   B Everyone knows an example of one.
   C They appeared at the same time as the Internet.
   D They're always about horrific events.

3 What does the author mean when he says 'the web is packed with fiction'?
   A You can find every story written online.
   B You can get most fiction for free online.
   C There are lots of stories on the Internet.
   D There are too many stories on the Internet.

4 What does the author suggest about urban legends in the last paragraph?
   A They're generally mystery stories.
   B They're usually short.
   C It's easier to discover if they're true or not.
   D Some include the author's name.

VOCABULARY

1 Complete the sentences with the words in the list. There are four extra words.

plot | setting | hero | character | opening | ending | villain | hilarious
miserable | terrified | fascinating | delighted | terrible | freezing

1 The _____ of the film is an amazing doctor who can travel through time and save people.
2 The show that we saw in the theatre last night was _____ . I couldn't stop laughing.
3 I've just read the last page of the book, and I don't like the _____ .
4 My brother can't swim. He's frightened of water and he's _____ of drowning.
5 He dived into the _____ water.
6 There is one _____ in the film who is really funny. He makes everybody laugh.
7 I haven't done my homework. I had a _____ headache last night.
8 The story was so sad that I felt _____ when I had finished reading it.
9 I'm _____ that you can come and see the show. The other actors will be happy too.
10 The _____ of the story is an evil vampire.

/10

GRAMMAR

2 Complete the sentences with the words / phrases in the list. There are two extra words / phrases.

are used | have it removed | have been taken | whose | where | who | that | are pulled

1 It's a story _____ has been passed down from generation to generation.
2 Hundreds of photos of the magician _____ .
3 She's an actress _____ has a great talent for storytelling.
4 Jack had a tattoo done a few years ago, and now he wants to _____ .
5 Two rabbits _____ out of a hat in this trick.
6 He still lives in the city _____ he was born.

3 Find and correct the mistake in each sentence.

1 The decision will be done by the judges tonight.
2 I didn't make very well in the test.
3 The marathon will have shown live on TV.
4 I won a medal for swimming last term, what made me feel proud.
5 I'm not allowed have my hair dyed.
6 Mrs Jones, who son I went to school with, is my piano teacher.

/12

FUNCTIONAL LANGUAGE

4 Circle the correct words.

1 A You'll never *know / believe* what happened just now.
   B *What / Really?*
   A I guessed all the answers in the TV quiz show correctly. What are the *chances / fates* of that?
2 A What's that song you keep singing?
   B That's the *annoying / angry* thing! I can't remember what it's called or who sings it.
3 A How does this machine work, then?
   B First, the engine *is / was* turned on. After *it / that,* the handbrake is released.
4 A I *had / made* my nose pierced yesterday. Do you like it?
   B No, I don't. And your dad's going to *kill / hurt* you when he sees it.

/8

MY SCORE /30

| 22 – 30 |
| 10 – 21 |
| 0 – 9 |

OBJECTIVES

FUNCTIONS: talking about permission; talking about habits; invitations

GRAMMAR: *make / let* and *be allowed to; be / get used to*

VOCABULARY: phrasal verbs (1); personality; phrases with *all*

READING

1 Look at the photos. What can you see? Use these words to help you.

skydiving | rugby | ironing

2 Answer the questions.

1 Do any of the photos make you laugh? Why?
2 Do you think any of the photos are strange? Why?
3 Do you think the photos have anything in common?

3 Read the film summary that your teacher tells you to read (A or B). Answer the questions.

1 Who is the main character in the film?
2 What does the main character really like doing?
3 Who makes things difficult for the main character?
4 Who (if anyone) helps the main character?
5 What happens at the end?

4 **SPEAKING** Work in pairs. Using your answers to Exercise 3, tell your partner about your film.

5 ◁) 2.03 Now read and listen to both summaries. Answer the questions.

1 Why doesn't Billy's dad want him to do ballet?
2 When does Billy's dad change his mind?
3 Where does the money come from for Billy to go to London?
4 Why don't Jess's parents let her play football?
5 When does Jess's dad change his mind?
6 What does Jess do to score the winning goal?

▮ TRAIN TO THiNK ▮

Thinking outside the box

In problem-solving, it can be useful to think really imaginatively, trying to avoid obvious or standard ideas. We call this 'thinking outside the box'. Sometimes thinking of very different possible answers to a problem helps us find the best solution.

It isn't a question of intelligence, just of thinking freely and creatively. The more you try it, the easier it is.

6 Complete the table with as many ideas as you can think of.

Questions about the films	My 'outside the box' ideas
1 Why does Billy's dad dislike Billy doing ballet?	*He hates the colour white. He was once attacked by a ballet dancer.*
2 How could Billy's dad get money for Billy to go to ballet school?	

7 How many 'outside the box' answers can you think of for these questions?

1 What weighs more than it did half a year ago?
2 What are things money can't buy?
3 What can you do at school but not at home?

A Billy Elliot

Billy Elliot is an 11-year-old boy who lives in the north of England. Billy's mother is dead, and he lives with his father and his brother, who are both coal miners.

Billy's father makes him <u>take up</u> boxing, but he hates it. One day, at the sports centre, Billy sees a group of girls doing ballet lessons and joins the class. But he doesn't tell his father, who believes that dancing is something that girls do, not boys. When Billy's father finds out about the ballet, he gets angry and he doesn't let his son take any more lessons. But Billy <u>carries on</u> in secret because he loves it.

Billy's ballet teacher, Georgia, encourages him to take a test to go to the Royal Ballet School in London. When she tells Billy's father, he says that Billy isn't allowed to dance any more. But then, one day, he sees Billy dancing. He realises that his son is talented, that it's his dream to go to the school in London and that he isn't going to <u>give up</u> dancing. After that, Billy's father does everything he can to help his son. He hasn't got any money, but other people in the town get the money together and then he takes Billy to London for the entrance test. Finally, Billy is accepted at the school and after years of study, he <u>ends up</u> as a top professional ballet dancer.

B Bend It Like Beckham

Jess Bhamra is the 18-year-old daughter of an Indian family in London. Jules Paxton is the same age and the daughter of an English family. Jess is crazy about football, but because she's a girl, she isn't allowed to play. Sometimes she plays in the park with some boys and one day, Jules, who also plays football, sees Jess playing. They <u>get on</u> really well and Jules invites Jess to try out for the local women's football team, coached by Joe. When he sees how good Jess is, Joe puts her in the team. When Jess's parents <u>find out</u> that she's been playing football without their knowing, they make her stop.

The team gets to an important final. Unfortunately, the final is on the same day as Jess's sister's wedding. Joe asks Mr Bhamra to let Jess play, but he refuses. Halfway through the wedding, Mr Bhamra lets Jess go. She rushes to the game.

When she <u>shows up</u>, there are only thirty minutes left and her team are losing 1–0. Soon, the score is 1–1, and when there's a free kick, Jess has to bend the ball around the other team's players to score. She makes it, and the team wins.

A university in California offers soccer scholarships to Jess and Jules. Jess finally convinces her parents to let her go. Jess and Jules <u>set off</u> for America and, later, they send a team photo to their families back home.

SPEAKING

Work in pairs. Discuss these questions.

1 If you haven't seen these films, which would you like to see? If you have seen them, which would you recommend?

2 Do you know any other films, books or true stories about someone who breaks a stereotype? Tell your partner.

GRAMMAR
make / let and *be allowed to*

1 **Complete these sentences from the film summaries on page 67. Then complete the rule with *make*, *let* and *be allowed to*.**

1 Billy's father _____ him take up boxing.
2 He _____ his son take any more lessons.
3 Billy _____ dance any more.
4 Because she's a girl, she _____ play.
5 They _____ her stop.
6 Joe asks Mr Bhamra to _____ Jess play.

> **RULE:** We can use [1]_____ (*someone do something*) and [2]_____ to talk about permission. We can use [3]_____ (*someone do something*) to talk about forcing someone to do something that they don't really want to do.

2 **Rewrite the sentences. Use each of the three structures at least once.**

0 I have to study every night. Dad says so.

Dad makes me study every night.

1 We can't eat food in the classroom.

_____

2 I can sleep late on Sundays. My parents say so.

_____

3 We have to read a book every week. The teacher says so.

_____

4 I can listen to music in my bedroom.

_____

5 We can wear our own clothes. The school says so.

_____

6 We can't play football in the garden. Mum says so.

_____

7 I don't have to go to bed early on Saturday. My parents say so.

_____

Workbook page 64 ▶

VOCABULARY
Phrasal verbs (1)

1 **Look at the <u>underlined</u> phrasal verbs in the film summaries on page 67. Match them with the definitions.**

1 begin a journey or trip
2 finally be in a situation or place (after some time or effort)
3 continue, not stop
4 start doing (an activity)
5 get information or learn about (something new)
6 arrive or appear at a place (usually late or unexpectedly)
7 stop (doing something)
8 have a good relationship, be friendly (with someone)

> **LOOK!** The verbs in Exercise 1 are examples of **phrasal verbs**. These are usually formed with an ordinary verb (for example, *take*) and a particle (for example, *up*): *take up*. Together, they have a particular meaning which is often quite different from the meaning of the verb alone.

2 **<u>Underline</u> the phrasal verbs in the sentences.**

1 I can't come tonight – I have to look after my little brother at home.
2 Do you know what time the plane takes off tomorrow?
3 I had fun last night – my friends came round and we watched a film.
4 She likes to hang out with her friends at the shopping centre.

3 **Complete the sentences with phrasal verbs from Exercises 1 and 2. Use the correct forms of the verbs.**

1 When we go on holiday, my friend _____ my pet rabbit.
2 I didn't like Jack when I met him, but now we're friends and we _____ really well.
3 She said she'd meet me at six o'clock, but she didn't _____ until seven.
4 Would you like to _____ to my house tonight?
5 I started learning Russian, but it was very difficult, so I _____ after six months.
6 I don't know what her name is, but I'm going to _____!
7 She hurt her foot, but she _____ playing until the end of the game.
8 I need to do more exercise, so I'm going to _____ running and cycling.

Workbook page 66 ▶

LISTENING

1 Write the words under the photos. Which country do you associate with these things?

bowing | sushi | underground | kimono | chopsticks

_____ _____ _____

2 **SPEAKING** What other things do you associate with this country? Compare your ideas.

3 2.04 Listen to a speaker describing her trip to Japan to some students. Which of the things in the photos does she mention?

4 2.04 Listen again. Mark the sentences T (true) or F (false).

According to the speaker, …

1 many European people think the Japanese are unfriendly. ☐

2 Japanese people are too polite. ☐

3 buses in England usually arrive on time. ☐

4 she usually eats with a knife and fork at home. ☐

5 she still doesn't know how to use chopsticks. ☐

6 you need an open mind when you go abroad. ☐

7 everyone in a country is the same. ☐

5 Think of two more questions about Japan. What do you think the speaker might say?

GRAMMAR
be / get used to

1 Complete these sentences from the listening. Use the phrases in the list. Then complete the rule with *infinitive* or *gerund*.

aren't used to | 'm used to
got used to | get used to

1 I _____ it very easily.

2 It was hard to _____ that.

3 We _____ buses arriving on time here.

4 I _____ eating with a knife and fork at home.

> **RULE:** *be / get used to* is followed by a noun or noun phrase, or by a verb in the _____ form. We use *be / get used to* (*doing*) *something* to talk about experience and habits. For example:
> *I'm hungry. **I'm not used to eating** so late.*
> *It was strange at first, but **I got used to it.***

> **LOOK!** *Be used to* refers to a **state** – something that is normal or familiar.
> *Get used to* refers to a **process** – something unusual *becomes* normal or familiar.

2 João is Brazilian, but he's living in London. Complete the sentences with the words.

~~traffic~~ | coats and jumpers | British money
sunshine | going | looking | weather
speaking | wearing | different accents

0 I'm from Rio, so I'm used to _traffic_ , but I'm not used to _____ right before I cross the road!

1 I haven't got used to the _____ yet. It rains a lot here. In Brazil, I was used to _____ .

2 It's hard to get used to all the _____! I'm not used to _____ so many clothes.

3 I'm used to _____ now. But most shops close at 5.30. I'm not used to _____ home so early.

4 I was used to _____ English before I arrived. But I'll never get used to all the _____ here.

Workbook page 65 ➤

READING

1 Look at the photos and the title. What do you think the article is about?

   A two men who built a prison

   B a man whose father went to prison and became president

   C a friendship between a prisoner and a prison warden

   D a friendship between two prisoners

2 Read the article quickly. Check your answer to Exercise 1.

My prisoner, my friend, my president and my father

In 1978, Christo Brand joined the prison service. He was an 18-year-old white South African boy [1]_____ . Now he was being sent to work as a warden in the famous prison on Robben Island. There, he was told, he was going to work with the biggest criminals in South African history, including political prisoners. Brand didn't know very much about politics – he just knew that he was going to work with some dangerous people.

And then he met prisoner 46664, a quiet 60-year-old black man who started to talk to Brand and ask him questions – questions about his family, his education, his plans for the future. Prisoner 46664 was Nelson Mandela, who would one day become the first black president of South Africa.

'There was no colour barrier between us,' said Brand, who later worked as a guide [2]_____ . 'Like me, Mandela came from a farm. We understood that we shared the same sky and the same air.' The two men got on well and became quite close, [3]_____ . They had to keep their friendship secret and their conversations had to be short. Brand found that Mandela was a warm and thoughtful person, [4]_____ .

Mandela was also a generous man, and he never forgot his friend. When he became president, he got Brand a job. One day, at a meeting of important politicians, Brand was in the room and was putting documents on the table. When Mandela came in, he saw Brand, went to him and hugged him. Mandela looked at all the people in the room and said, '[5]_____ . This person was my friend.' Brand says that he felt very proud at that moment.

Nelson Mandela died in December 2013, aged 95. Like so many people around the world, Brand was very sad [6]_____ . He said at the time, 'Mandela was my prisoner, my friend, my president and my father.'

3 Read the article again and match phrases a–g with spaces 1–6. There's one extra phrase which doesn't belong in the article.

   a even a little shy sometimes

   b when he heard the news

   c who had grown up on a farm

   d showing tourists around Robben Island

   e hoping to become his friend

   f This person was my warden

   g although this wasn't allowed by the prison authorities

4 Answer the questions.

   1 Where did Brand spend his childhood?

   2 What kind of prisoners was Brand told he was going to work with?

   3 What did Brand and Mandela have in common?

   4 Why did Mandela and Brand have to keep their friendship secret?

   5 What did Mandela do for Brand when he became president?

VOCABULARY
Personality

1 Read the sentences about the listening on page 69 and the article on page 70. (Circle) the correct words.

1 Some people in Europe think that the Japanese are *cold and unfriendly / lively and polite*.

2 The woman who went to Japan thought the Japanese were *selfish and rude / warm and kind*.

3 The writer describes Mandela as a *lively and selfish / generous and thoughtful* man.

2 Use a dictionary to check the meaning of any of the words in Exercise 1 that you are unsure of.

3 Which adjectives are positive, negative and neutral? Mark them +, – or 0.

4 Which adjectives describe each person? You can choose more than one for each person.

1 No, it's mine. You can't use it.

2 I don't want to go to the party, thanks. I'm not comfortable with strangers.

3 Jack's had some bad news. Let's go and talk to him. Perhaps he needs a friend.

4 Don't worry. There's a problem, but everything's going to be all right, OK?

5 Go away! I'm working. I don't want to talk to you now.

5 Complete each response with an adjective. There may be more than one possible answer.

1 A Hey, you! Get out of my way!
   B What a _____ boy!

2 A The children aren't tired at all.
   B Yes, they're very _____ tonight.

3 A Let's all go and have a hamburger. I'll pay.
   B Wow! That's very _____ of you.

4 A He always says 'please' and 'thank you'.
   B Yes, he's very _____ .

5 A She never laughs or cries or anything.
   B I know. She's a bit _____ sometimes.

6 A Mandy always thinks about other people.
   B Yes, she's a really _____ person.

6 Write four sentences about people you know. (You don't need to use their names!) Use adjectives from Exercise 1 and give reasons.

I know someone who I think is rude because he/she never says hello at the bus stop.

7 SPEAKING Compare your sentences with the class.

Workbook page 66

■ THiNK VALUES ■
Stereotypes

1 SPEAKING Work in small groups. Discuss these questions.

stereotype: a fixed idea about what groups of people are like

1 Think about your own country, or a region of your country. Do people from other places have fixed ideas about the people who live there?

Some people think the British aren't very friendly but that they're very polite.

2 Why do you think people have these ideas?

3 Do you think there is any truth in the stereotypes of your country or region?

2 Some stereotypes are about nationalities. What other groups of people are there stereotypes about? Write a list. Then compare your ideas.

people who live in small towns

3 In your groups, discuss stereotypes that you think people have about teenagers.

WRITING
An article about stereotypes

Write an article (80–120 words) for a school magazine about a national stereotype. Think about:

- a culture that some people in your country see as a stereotype.

In Britain, a lot of people think that Americans talk very loudly, only eat fast food and wear colourful clothes.

- why you think the stereotype exists.

I think it's because some American tourists in Britain are a bit like that sometimes, and in some films too.

- why this stereotype is wrong.

My friend went to the USA last year. She said she ate excellent food and the Americans she met were quiet and stylishly dressed!

The nerd

1 **Look at the photos and answer the questions.**

Who are they all talking about?
What do you think Flora's problem is?

2 ◄))2.05 **Now read and listen to the photostory. Check your answers.**

JEFF Don't look now, but Richie Ford's sitting behind you.
LEO Let me guess: he's doing something on his computer.
JEFF Got it in one.
LEO He spends all day on that thing.
JEFF I know. Hasn't he got a life?
FLORA Pack it in, you two. You're being mean.
MIA Yeah, and he can probably hear what you're saying.
JEFF No, it's all right. He's got his earphones in. He's such a nerd.
FLORA Oh, come on, Jeff. That isn't nice.
JEFF I didn't say there's anything wrong with being a nerd.
MIA No, but that's what you meant.
JEFF No, it isn't.
FLORA Then why use that word?
MIA Just because he's into computers and he wears glasses, it doesn't mean he's a nerd.
LEO I'm with you on this one, Jeff.
MIA What does that mean exactly?
LEO Don't get me wrong. I've got nothing against nerds. After all, my brother's one! But Richie Ford is most definitely a nerd.
JEFF Yeah, all we're saying is that he should get off the computer now and then and actually meet some people.
FLORA And how do you know he hasn't got lots of friends?
JEFF Well, yes, OK – for all I know he's got loads of friends somewhere. But he's always on his own at school.
LEO That isn't true at all. He's got his best friend: his computer.
FLORA Sometimes I just don't know why I'm friends with you two.
MIA Boys. They're all the same.

LEO Sorry, Flora, I can't help you with this one. Error code 324, you say? I've never even heard of that one before.
FLORA Oh, no, Leo. You were my only hope. Ugh, this computer!
LEO Now, if you were friends with Richie Ford, of course ...
FLORA Stop that. It isn't funny. And anyway, if you knew as much as him, then maybe you *would* be able to help.
LEO Yeah, good point. I'll shut up.
FLORA So what am I going to do about my computer?
LEO Take it in and have it fixed, I suppose. There's that new computer shop down Brook Street. I hear they're really good.
FLORA Yeah, I'll have to take it in tomorrow. I'm so tired of all the problems I keep having with this computer. I want to get it fixed once and for all. Thanks for trying, anyway.
LEO Don't mention it. Hope they can fix it.

DEVELOPING SPEAKING

3 Work in pairs. Discuss what happens next in the story. Write down your ideas.

We think Flora asks Richie to fix her computer.

4 ◘◄ EP3 Watch and find out how the story continues.

5 Answer the questions.

Who …

1 fixes Flora's computer?
2 invites Flora to go climbing?
3 decides not to go climbing?
4 is late for the first lesson?
5 is climbing the wall when they arrive at the sports centre?

PHRASES FOR FLUENCY

1 Find these expressions in the photostory. Who says them? How do you say them in your language?

1 Got it in one.
2 Pack it in.
3 I'm with you on this one.
4 Don't get me wrong.
5 Good point.
6 Don't mention it.

2 Use the expressions in Exercise 1 to complete the conversation.

TOM Did you use my laptop without asking me?

MIKE No, I didn't.

TOM Well, I think you did. Dad, can you please tell Mike to ask first?

DAD ¹_____ . I want everyone in the car in five minutes.

TOM Where are we going? Shopping?

DAD ²_____ !

TOM Again?! Do we have to?

MIKE ³_____ , Tom. Can't we stay at home? We'll only moan and make life difficult for you and Mum if we come.

DAD Actually, that's a ⁴_____ .

MIKE I mean, ⁵_____ . It isn't that we don't like being with you and Mum …

DAD No, you two can stay behind and tidy up the house.

TOM Oh, great. Thanks, Dad!

DAD ⁶_____ . And no fighting!

WordWise
Phrases with *all*

1 Complete these sentences from the photostory with the expressions.

after all | all day | once and for all
for all I know | all we're saying | all the same

1 He spends _____ on that thing.
2 I've got nothing against nerds. _____ , my brother's one!
3 Yeah, _____ is that he should get off the computer now and then.
4 Well, yes, OK – _____ he's got loads of friends somewhere.
5 Boys. They're _____ .
6 I want to get it fixed _____ .

2 Replace the underlined phrases with expressions from Exercise 1.

1 He's here from the morning to the evening.
2 I suppose it's possible that he's really nice.
3 Of course I like Italian food – as an example to prove my point, I eat pizza, don't I?
4 The point we're making is that he's a bit lazy.
5 Girls are always like this.
6 I've solved the problem so it never happens again.

> Workbook page 66 ➤

FUNCTIONS
Invitations

1 Complete the sentences with the words in the list.

about | would | count | don't | fancy | love | course

1 Why _____ you come along?
2 How _____ bringing some friends along with you?
3 Do you _____ coming along?
4 That _____ be fantastic. I'd _____ to.
5 Yes, of _____ . It's a great idea.
6 You'll have to _____ me out.

2 ROLE PLAY Work in pairs. Student A: turn to page 127. Student B: turn to page 128.

Pronunciation

Intonation – inviting, accepting and refusing invitations

Go to page 121.

OBJECTIVES

FUNCTIONS: reporting what someone said, asked or requested; giving and reacting to news

GRAMMAR: reported speech (review); reported questions, requests and imperatives

VOCABULARY: crime; reporting verbs

READING

1 Look at the words for different types of criminals. How do you say them in your language?

1 burglar
2 con man
3 mugger
4 pickpocket
5 robber
6 shoplifter

2 Match the pictures with the words from Exercise 1.

A

B

C

D

E

F

3 Think of examples of these criminals from the news, books, TV or films.

4 Look at the photos on page 75 and the headlines. Guess what the news stories are about. Then read and check.

5 🔊 2.08 Read the news stories again and listen. Answer the questions. Write *Mrs Atkins* or *Mr Caron*.

Who …

0 discovered something was missing? *Mrs Atkins*

1 didn't get what he'd/she'd requested? _____

2 was the victim of a con man? _____

3 decided to get in touch with the criminal? _____

4 has forgiven the criminal? _____

5 had been a bit careless? _____

6 was the victim of a theft? _____

■ TRAIN TO THiNK ■

Thinking about empathy

To understand another person's feelings, you need to 'put yourself in their shoes' – try to imagine how you'd feel in their situation.

6 Read the first story again. Who do you think felt these emotions? Match 1–3 with a–c.

1 Mrs Atkins ☐
2 the thief ☐
3 the reporter ☐

a sympathetic when he/she heard the story
b guilty when he/she read the note
c sad when he/she thought about all the fun he'd/she'd had on the bike

7 Read the second story again. How do you think these people felt and why?

the children | his wife
the reporter | the con man

Thief feels sorry

When teacher Margaret Atkins, 49, went to ride her bike to school last Friday, she was shocked to discover it wasn't there. When our reporter spoke to her, she told him that she'd been really angry when she realised the bike was gone. She said a friend had given it to her years ago and that it was quite an old bike, but that she'd always liked it.

So what did she do? She decided to write a note to the thief and put it on the tree next to the bike stand that it had been stolen from. To her surprise, when she came back from school the same day, she found the thief had returned the bike, together with a written apology. 'I'm sorry I stole your bike. What I did was wrong. I've replaced the lock as I'd broken it. Hope you can accept my apology!'

The next morning, Mrs Atkins told reporters that she was still feeling surprised at what had happened. She said that although most people would be angry in her situation, she was just grateful that she could go to school on her bike again. Mrs Atkins added that she'd probably write another message to the thief. 'I want to thank him for returning the bike and tell him I've forgiven him,' she explained. She said that she wasn't going to report the incident to the police because she believed everyone could do bad things sometimes. 'What counts is that people own up to their mistakes,' she said.

SHARE ◉ ✉   COMMENTS

Father angry victim of online con

Frank Caron, 29, will think twice before using his credit card online again. Caron spent £450 on what he thought was the popular Xbox One console, a birthday present for his twins Mia and Michael, seven. When he found out that he'd been tricked, he was the 'maddest man in town', as he told our reporter.

Mr Caron said that the family's financial situation was difficult, as most of their money went to pay the mortgage on their house. But he added that the twins had desperately wanted the games console and he and his wife had been proud to get them the toy they wanted. He said they'd seen the console on a well-known shopping auction website months ago and had thought it was a bargain. He started saving up for it immediately, and hoped nobody else would buy it before he had the money. He said he'd been absolutely furious when he opened the box and all he found inside was a low-resolution photo of the games console he'd wanted to buy.

When Mr Caron went online to understand how he'd been tricked, he realised he'd been the victim of an online scam, a modern-day con. He said that he'd felt furious when he re-read the seller's advertisement: 'Xbox One console, top model photo, brand new'.

SHARE ◉ ✉   COMMENTS

SPEAKING

Work in pairs. Discuss these questions.

1   What do you think of Mrs Atkins's reaction when …
   a   she noticed her bike was stolen?   b   she found the thief's note?
   How would you have reacted in those situations?
2   What things (if any) do you buy online? Have you or has anyone you know ever been scammed?

GRAMMAR
Reported speech (review)

1 **Complete the sentences with suitable verbs. Then check your answers in the news stories on page 75.**

1 She told him that she _____ really angry.
2 She said a friend _____ it to her years ago.
3 She said that […] she _____ it.
4 She said that she _____ still _____ surprised.
5 She said that […] most people _____ angry in her situation.
6 She said she was grateful that she _____ to school on her bike again.
7 She added that she _____ probably _____ another message.
8 She said that she _____ the incident to the police.

2 **Match what Mrs Atkins said (direct speech) with the reported sentences in Exercise 1. <u>Underline</u> the verb forms which are different. Then complete the rule.**

a 'I've always liked it.'
b 'I'm still feeling surprised.'
c 'I was really angry!'
d 'I'm grateful that I can go to school on my bike again.'
e 'Most people would be angry in my situation.'
f 'I'm not going to report the incident to the police.'
g 'A friend gave it to me years ago.'
h 'I'll probably write another message.'

RULE:

Direct speech		Reported speech
present simple	→	0 *past simple*
present continuous	→	1 _____
present perfect	→	2 _____
past simple	→	3 _____
past perfect	→	4 _____
would	→	5 _____
can	→	6 _____
will	→	7 _____
am / is / are going to	→	8 _____

3 **Rewrite these sentences in reported speech.**

1 'I'd be happy to put cameras all over the shop,' the manager said.
2 'The police can't find the con man,' Dad said.
3 'We saw the robber from across the street,' the woman told the police.
4 'We're thinking of having a new alarm installed,' the shop owner said.
5 'We haven't heard or seen anything,' our neighbours said.
6 'I'll buy the games console for you,' the man told his kids.

Workbook page 72

VOCABULARY
Crime

1 **Match the words with the definitions.**

to murder | to break in | to arrest | a fine
to commit a crime | to go to prison | a murderer
to get into trouble | to get caught | a prisoner

1 to do something illegal
2 to be made to live in a special building for criminals
3 to take (a suspected criminal) to the police station
4 to kill (a person) intentionally
5 money that you have to pay if you break a law
6 to enter by force (usually to steal something)
7 someone who intentionally kills another person
8 to be found while committing a crime
9 to have a problem because of something that you did wrong
10 a person who is in prison

2 **SPEAKING Work in pairs. Use these questions to help you invent a crime story. Make notes and then tell your partner your story.**

- Where and when did it happen?
- Who was involved?
- What happened?
- What crime was committed?
- How did the police react?
- What happened to the criminal?

Workbook page 74

LISTENING

1 SPEAKING Imagine a young person mugged somebody. Discuss these questions.

1 Why might someone mug a person?
2 Who might suffer as a result?
3 What would be the best punishment?

2 2.09 Listen to a radio interview. What is Restoring Justice and who is it for?

3 2.09 Listen again and make notes on these topics.

1 Jason's initial reaction to Restoring Justice
2 The main idea behind Restoring Justice
3 How Jason felt about meeting his victim
4 How Mrs Schwartz felt about meeting her mugger
5 The reason Jason gave for mugging Mrs Schwartz
6 The people Mrs Schwartz feels suffered most

GRAMMAR
Reported questions, requests and imperatives

1 Match 1–4 with a–d. Then complete the rule with *asked*, *if*, *told* and *whether*.

1 She asked me if I knew who'd suffered
2 [The judge] asked me whether I wanted
3 [She] asked me to look at the other side
4 He told me to

a think carefully about my choices.
b to go to prison.
c of the table, where my mum and dad were sitting.
d most from what I'd done.

> **RULE:**
> • In reported **yes / no questions**, we use *asked* + ¹_____ or _____ and the same word order as in a statement.
> • In reported **requests**, we use ²_____ + object + infinitive.
> • In reported **imperatives**, we use ³_____ + object + infinitive.

2 These are things people have said to Ken, the social worker. Rewrite them in reported speech.

0 Reporter: 'Have you had much success with the programme so far?'
The reporter asked if he'd had much success with the programme so far.

1 Presenter: 'Are victims scared of meeting their muggers?'
2 Ken's wife: 'Did you see the article about Restoring Justice in the newspaper this morning?'
3 Presenter: 'Could you tell us more about the ideas behind the programme, please?'
4 Ken's manager: 'Don't include other criminals in the programme.'

3 Write 4–6 more questions that Mrs Schwartz might ask Jason. Use direct speech. Then put your partner's questions into reported speech.

'How do you see your future?'
She asked him how he saw his future.

Workbook page 73

■ THiNK VALUES ■

Respecting the law; understanding that punishment will follow crime

1 Match the punishments 1–6 with a–f.

1 He got **a fine**.
2 He got **community service**.
3 He got **a life sentence**.
4 He got **a caution**.
5 He got **the death penalty**.
6 He got **a prison sentence**.

a He has to spend 80 hours cleaning the streets.
b But he'll be in serious trouble if he does it again.
c It means at least 20 years in prison.
d But it will be years before they carry it out.
e He had to pay £100.
f He'll be inside for two years.

2 Number the punishments in Exercise 1 from 1 (least serious) to 6 (most serious).

3 SPEAKING Work in pairs. Read these newspaper headlines. What crimes have been committed? What punishment (if any) would be fair?

• Hungry student steals chocolate bar from shop
• Man steals TV from old couple's home
• Speeding driver kills family of four
• Bank robber escapes with thousands

READING

1 Read the article quickly. Which *two* ideas to help prevent crime does it mention?

GETTING CREATIVE with crime

CYCLE THIEVES WE ARE WATCHING YOU

Newcastle University Estate Security Service in partnership with Northumbria Police

OPERATION CRACKDO

An experiment carried out at Newcastle University aimed at reducing the number of bike thefts has produced some remarkable results. The most efficient way of stopping people from stealing bikes seems almost too simple to be true. If you want to persuade thieves not to act, make them feel they're being watched!

Posters showing a large pair of eyes were put up near three bike racks at the university, while other bike racks had no posters. The researchers explained that the number of thefts decreased by 62 per cent compared to the previous year at racks with posters. However, at the other racks, thefts actually increased by 63 per cent. Experts claim that clearly visible images of eyes make people feel they're being watched. They say that we all care what other people think about us and that's why we behave better when we think someone is looking. Now officials have agreed to carry out similar projects at train stations all over the country.

The 'giant eyes' poster isn't the only unusual method being used to try and fight crime on UK streets. In the East Midlands city of Leicester, police are inviting people to make large woolly balls and hang them up in trees around the area. They hope that these colourful additions to neighbourhoods will help create a safer place to live. The thinking behind the idea is that if you create a pleasant environment, people are more likely to behave better. 'We live in a world where our every move is being watched by CCTV cameras,' one of the organisers told us. 'The cameras are there to deter possible criminals, but they come at a price, and many people don't like being watched 24 hours a day. We believe there's another way. We want to encourage people to take more pride in where they live.'

However, not all residents are happy – many refuse to believe it will make any difference. They're demanding that the police do more to reduce trouble in the area. One local resident told us, 'I recommend that the police stop wasting their time on mad schemes like this and do some real policing. We need to see more policemen walking around our streets, especially at night.'

2 Read the article again and mark the sentences T (true) or F (false).

1 The crime prevention scheme at Newcastle University used the latest technology.
2 After the posters were put up, there were fewer bike thefts from all the university bike racks.
3 There are plans to use the posters in other parts of the UK.
4 It's hoped that the woolly balls will make people care more about where they live.
5 CCTV cameras will be used to catch criminals interfering with the woolly balls.
6 The woolly ball scheme is popular with all residents.

3 **SPEAKING** Work in pairs. Discuss these questions.

1 What do you think about each of the ideas in the text?
2 What other crime prevention schemes have you heard of?

VOCABULARY
Reporting verbs

1 Complete the sentences with the correct forms of the verbs. Then check your answers in the article on page 78.

explain | encourage | demand | persuade
invite | recommend | claim | refuse | agree

1 If you want to _____ thieves not to act, make them feel they're being watched!

2 The researchers _____ that the number of thefts decreased by 62 per cent …

3 Experts _____ that clearly visible images of eyes make people feel they're being watched.

4 Now officials have _____ to carry out similar projects at train stations.

5 Police are _____ people to make large woolly balls.

6 We want to _____ people to take more pride in where they live.

7 Not all residents are happy – many _____ to believe it will make any difference.

8 They're _____ that the police do more to reduce trouble in the area.

9 I _____ that the police stop wasting their time on mad schemes like this.

2 Match the verbs with the definitions.

1 agree ☐ 4 demand ☐
2 claim ☐ 5 persuade ☐
3 explain ☐ 6 refuse ☐

a make something clear
b try to get someone to do or believe something
c accept an idea or a suggestion
d say no
e insist something is done
f say that something is true

3 Complete the rule with reporting verbs from Exercises 1 and 2.

> **RULE:** We use different structures with different reporting verbs.
>
> 1 verb + infinitive with (not) to
>   *agree, offer,* _____
>
> 2 verb + object + infinitive with (not) to
>   *ask, tell,* _____ , _____ , _____
>
> 3 verb + that + clause
>   *say, claim,* _____ , _____ , _____
>
> 4 verb + gerund
>   *apologise for, suggest*

4 Complete the sentences with the correct forms of the verbs and any other necessary words.

1 Liam agreed _____ (meet) me at nine o'clock.
2 Lucy apologised _____ (forget) my birthday.
3 Jack refused _____ (help) us.
4 Bobby persuaded _____ (me / go) to the party with him.
5 Dad suggested _____ (have) dinner at a restaurant.
6 My mum encouraged _____ (me / enter) the singing competition.
7 Mr Jones recommended _____ (we / read) the book before we saw the film.
8 Liz offered _____ (drive) me home after the match.

5 Rewrite the sentences in reported speech. Use suitable reporting verbs. Sometimes more than one verb is possible.

1 'We forgot to inform you. We're really sorry,' they said.
2 'We're going to introduce a new system to reduce crime,' the mayor said.
3 'Can you give us more information about the plan?' the reporter said to the official.
4 'If you work for us, you'll be very rich soon,' the man said.
5 'I don't want to buy the watch because it's too expensive,' the woman said.
6 'Study this text carefully!' the teacher said to the class.
7 'I can help you with your work,' the man said.
8 'Come to my office tomorrow morning, please,' the headmaster said to my parents.
9 'Oh, all right. I'll go to the cinema with you, but only if you pay,' Jack said to Olivia.

Workbook page 74 ▶

WRITING
A report of a crime

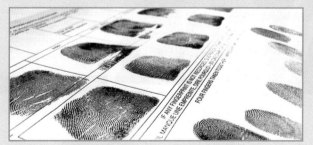

Write a newspaper report about a crime (100–150 words).

- Give a description of the crime (what happened).
- Include what one witness said.
- Say what the investigators think.

Culture

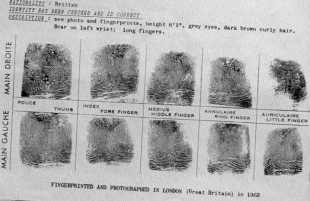

1 Scan the article and answer the questions.

1 What crime did each of these men commit?

2 What punishment did each of them get?

2 🔊 2.10 Read and listen to the article. Check your answers.

Famous criminals

What do these three men have in common? All are, or were, incredibly rich at some point in their lives. However, there's little to admire in their apparent success – they all got their money in deeply dishonest ways.

One of the most common ways of stealing money these days is to steal it from your company. It's called embezzlement and **Dennis Kozlowski** was very good at it! Kozlowski was a top manager at an American company named Tyco a few years ago. (Ironically, one of the company's most recognised brands is ADT Home Security.) Kozlowski and another senior manager decided to help themselves to the company's money. It was a lot of money, and Kozlowski wasn't afraid to spend it! He bought a house costing $19 million and an apartment in New York for $18 million. He even spent $2 million on a private concert from the singer Jimmy Buffet. Altogether, he managed to steal $600 million before someone noticed. He's now in prison and has a lot of time to think about his 'success'.

Ronald Biggs was involved in the Great Train Robbery of 1963. Early one morning, a gang of men stopped a train in the British countryside.

They hit the train driver over the head and drove the train towards a bridge. A lorry was waiting underneath, and they dropped 120 mailbags of money from the train into it. They then drove to a farm nearby and shared out the money. Biggs got £147,000, which was a fortune at the time. When the police later found the farm, Biggs's fingerprints were all over the place. He was caught and sent to prison, but escaped after fifteen months. Biggs avoided British justice for almost 40 years, living in Australia and then in Brazil. He returned to Britain in 2001 because of bad health and died in 2013.

American **Albert Gonzalez**, also called 'The Hacker', worked for the US Secret Service in the early 2000s, trying to catch cybercriminals. But he didn't stay on that side of the law for long, and soon formed his own gang of hackers. They planned to make millions, and they did. The gang hacked into the computer networks of huge retail stores. They managed to steal the details of 140 million credit cards, and sold them to criminal organisations in other countries. They were successful for some time, but an international police operation finally tracked them down. Gonzalez was sentenced to 20 years in prison, but his victims had lost millions of dollars.

3 Answer the questions.

1 How did Dennis Kozlowski get his money?

2 How did he spend it?

3 How did Ronnie Biggs get his money?

4 How did he get caught?

5 How did Albert Gonzalez get his money?

6 What prison sentence did he get?

4 SPEAKING Work in pairs. Discuss these questions.

1 What other famous crimes do you know of?

2 What do you think should be done to stop cybercrime?

5 **VOCABULARY** There are eight highlighted words or phrases in the article. Match them with these definitions.

1 a group of criminals who work together
2 found out where they were
3 close, not far away
4 people who suffer because of a criminal act
5 stealing from the business or organisation you work for
6 take (without asking)
7 everywhere
8 shops

LISTENING

1 🔊 2.11 Listen to the conversations and match them with the photos.

A ☐

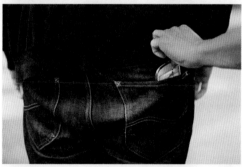

B ☐

C ☐

D ☐

2 🔊 2.11 Listen again and complete the notes.

> Conversation 1
> Crime: _____ What was taken: _____
>
> Conversation 2
> Crime: _____ What was taken: _____
>
> Conversation 3
> Crime: _____ What was taken: _____
>
> Conversation 4
> Crime: _____ What was taken: _____

FUNCTIONS
Giving and reacting to news

1 Put the words in order to form expressions for giving news from the conversations.

1 never / You'll / what / guess
2 believe / won't / to / week / what / You / happened / last / me
3 about / a / really / an / sad / lady / story / heard / I / old
4 paper / a / scary / story / There / the / was / other / in / day / the

2 Complete the reactions to news.

1 T__ll m__.
2 Wh__t?
3 R__ __lly?
4 Th__t's __wf__l!
5 N__ w__y!

3 Work in pairs. Make conversations using the expressions from Exercises 1 and 2.

• Think of (or make up) a piece of news.
• Take turns to give your news.
• React and ask for more details.

> **Pronunciation**
> Intonation – expressing surprise
> **Go to page 121.**

READING AND USE OF ENGLISH
Part 3: Word formation

Workbook page 71

1   For questions 1–7, read the text below. Use the word given in capitals at the end of some of the lines to form a word that fits in the gap in the same line. There is an example at the beginning (0).

A thief who kissed his victim after a **(0)** _robbery_ in a   ROB
French jewellery shop has been caught after a forensic
(1) _____ matched his DNA with that left on the   SCIENCE
hand of his victim.
The thief **(2)** _____ the Parisian shop late in the   ENTRY
afternoon, as the owner was preparing to close for the
evening. After tying the woman to a chair, he
smashed open **(3)** _____ display cabinets and   VARY
loaded **(4)** _____ worth more than 20,000 euros   VALUE
into a bag. Before leaving the shop, he kissed the owner's
hand and made an **(5)** _____ for his crime.   APOLOGISE
However, the **(6)** _____ thief could never have   LUCK
imagined that the kiss would lead to his arrest. Police
used the DNA and ran it through a database of all known
(7) _____ .   CRIME

WRITING
Part 2: An informal email

Workbook page 79

2   You have received an email from an English-speaking penfriend.

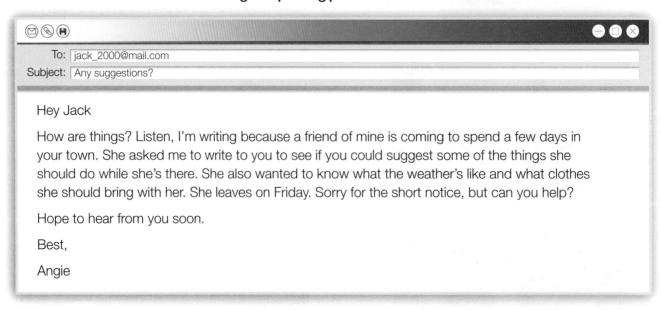

To: jack_2000@mail.com
Subject: Any suggestions?

Hey Jack

How are things? Listen, I'm writing because a friend of mine is coming to spend a few days in your town. She asked me to write to you to see if you could suggest some of the things she should do while she's there. She also wanted to know what the weather's like and what clothes she should bring with her. She leaves on Friday. Sorry for the short notice, but can you help?

Hope to hear from you soon.

Best,

Angie

Write your email in 140–190 words.

VOCABULARY

1 **Complete the sentences with the words / phrases in the list. There are four extra words / phrases.**

give up | got into trouble | unfriendly | generous | find out | after all
commit a crime | calm | selfish | set off | burglar | shy | arrested | end up

1 Don't _____ now. You're a great player. I'm sure you'll get on the team next time.
2 That was very _____ of you to eat all those cakes and not leave any for us.
3 We _____ very early in the morning because we wanted to arrive before it got dark.
4 Tim _____ for not doing his English homework again.
5 The _____ broke into the house when everybody was asleep.
6 I hope they _____ who stole Amanda's purse.
7 It was very _____ of James to pay for all your concert tickets.
8 It rained a lot that day, so we didn't go on the school trip _____ .
9 The police finally _____ the con man and he went to prison.
10 Emma doesn't find it easy to meet new people. She's very _____ .

/10

GRAMMAR

2 **Complete the sentences with the words / phrases in the list. There are two extra words / phrases.**

get used to | would | 'm not used to | going to | encouraged | is | had been | got used to

1 My mum _____ me to do well at school.
2 The policeman told me that the thief _____ get a prison sentence.
3 I _____ taking my shoes off before I go into a house, but here in Japan, it's what everyone does.
4 She says she is _____ report the crime to the police.
5 At home, I always have dinner at six o'clock, so I haven't _____ eating at nine o'clock here in Spain.
6 She said the con man _____ sentenced to two years in prison.

3 **Find and correct the mistake in each sentence.**

1 She asked me if I knew who has taken the bike.
2 My mum let me do all the washing-up for a week because I was late home one night.
3 He persuaded me report the theft to the police.
4 I really want to go on the school trip, but my dad won't make me.
5 The reporter explained me that the mugger would get community service.
6 My parents make me to tidy my bedroom.

/12

FUNCTIONAL LANGUAGE

4 **Circle the correct words.**

1 A We're going camping this weekend. Why don't you come *along / on*?
  B I'd love to. How *for / about* asking Mike to come too?
2 A We're going swimming. Does anyone *feel / fancy* coming along?
  B You can *call / count* me out. I hate swimming.
3 A The other day I *hear / heard* a really sad story about an old man whose house was burgled.
  B *That's / It's* awful!

/8

4 A You'll never *believe / understand* what happened to me last week!
  B Go on then. *Say / Tell* me!

MY SCORE | **/30**

| 22 – 30 |
| 10 – 21 |
| 0 – 9 |

OBJECTIVES

FUNCTIONS: making deductions
GRAMMAR: modals of deduction (present); *should(n't) have*; modals of deduction (past)
VOCABULARY: mysteries; expressions with *go*

A

B

C

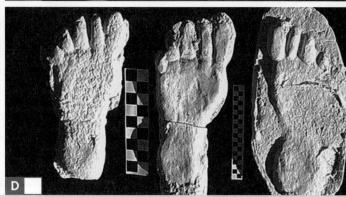

D

READING

1 **Look at the photos and match them with the mysteries.**

the yeti | the Loch Ness monster | crop circles | UFOs

2 **SPEAKING** **Work in pairs. Compare your answers. What do you know about these mysteries?**

3 **Read the article quickly. Why *isn't* the author writing about any of the mysteries in Exercise 1?**

4 🔊 2.14 **Read the article again and listen.**
✱ **Answer the questions.**

Which mystery…
1 involves the possible ancient use of modern technology?
2 involves an object found in Asia?
3 involves the oldest object?
4 hasn't been connected with alien activity?
5 was discovered in a really old city?
6 started half a century ago?
7 came from under the earth?
8 involves a round object with strange patterns on it?

■ TRAIN TO THiNK ■

Fact or opinion?

A fact is something that can be proven to be true.
An opinion is a personal belief. It's important to be able to see the difference.

5 **Read about the Nampa Doll again. According to what is written in the text, mark the sentences F (fact) or O (opinion).**

1 The doll was found in Nampa. ☐
2 It was 100m below the earth. ☐
3 It's from an ancient civilisation. ☐
4 It's from another planet. ☐

6 **Complete the table with two facts and two opinions for each mystery according to the article.**

	Fact	Opinion
Teotihuacan		
The Suicide Dog Bridge		
The Lolladoff Plate		

The truth is out there

There are many unexplained mysteries in the world. How was the Great Pyramid at Giza built? How are crop circles made? Are there yetis in the Himalayas? Have we been visited by extraterrestrials? And is there a sea monster in the depths of Loch Ness? But other, less well known phenomena are equally mysterious. Here are our favourites.

1 The Nampa Doll

In July 1889, in Nampa, Idaho, USA, a man named M.A. Kurtz was drilling a well in the ground when he noticed the drill had brought up a strange small brown object from under the earth. When he looked more closely, he found it was a figure made from clay. Amazingly, it had come from almost 100 metres below the surface, suggesting that it was more than 300,000 years old. In other words, it appeared to be from a time before humans walked on the Earth. So how did it get there? Some people say it could be evidence of an ancient lost civilisation. Others are sure it must be extraterrestrial. Whatever the truth, it makes you wonder how much we really know about our past.

2 Teotihuacan

Over 2,000 years ago, Teotihuacan in central Mexico was one of the largest cities in the world. It is especially famous for its incredible Mesoamerican pyramids, although these days not much of it remains. However, scientists exploring the ruins were amazed to find large amounts of the mineral mica in the city walls. The nearest place where mica is found is thousands of kilometres away, in Brazil. Nowadays, mica is important in the production of energy. Did the inhabitants of Teotihuacan know this secret? And is that why they went to so much trouble to bring it all the way from South America?

3 The Suicide Dog Bridge

The Overtoun Bridge near Milton in Scotland is famous for a sad reason. Over the last 50 years, 50 dogs have died, all jumping from a similar point on the bridge. But what is the reason for this puzzling phenomenon? Most animal experts agree that the dogs can't be committing suicide because they don't have such complex feelings, although some people think the dogs might sense their owners' unhappiness and jump for them. Others think the bridge is haunted. Perhaps the best explanation is that the dogs can smell the nests of minks below and, in trying to catch these small animals, are jumping without thinking.

4 The Lolladoff Plate

The 12,000-year-old Lolladoff plate was found in Nepal. The story goes that just after the Second World War, a Polish professor was travelling through Northern India and bought the plate at a local market. He was told it was from a secret race of people called the Dzopa, who used it for religious ceremonies. The plate is marked with spiral lines, odd symbols and a grey figure – according to UFO fans, an alien being. In fact, the plate looks just like a flying saucer. Some people claim that it is proof that aliens have already walked on the Earth. Others say the plate can't be genuine and is a fake.

SPEAKING

Work in pairs. Discuss these questions.

1 Which of these mysteries do you think is the most interesting? Why?
2 What other mysteries do you know of?

Pronunciation
Moving word stress
Go to page 121.

GRAMMAR
Modals of deduction (present)

1   Complete the sentences from the article on page 85. Use *must*, *can't*, *could* and *might*. Then complete the rule.

  1 Some people say it _____ be evidence of an ancient lost civilisation.

  2 Others are sure it _____ be extraterrestrial.

  3 Some people think the dogs _____ sense their owners' unhappiness and jump for them.

  4 Others say the plate _____ be genuine.

> **RULE:**
> - When we're sure something is true, we use [1]_____ .
> - When we're sure something *isn't* true, we use [2]_____ .
> - When we aren't so sure, we use [3]_____ or _____ to express doubt.

2   Complete the sentences with suitable modal verbs. Sometimes there's more than one possible answer.

  1 They're speaking Spanish, so they _____ be from Argentina, I suppose.

  2 She _____ love cats – she's got 20.

  3 You _____ want more – you've already eaten two whole pizzas!

  4 I'm not sure, but I think that man _____ need our help. I don't think he can swim.

  5 You've been working all day. You _____ feel really tired.

  6 He's a bit older than John, but he _____ know him. I think they went to the same school.

  7 Tim _____ be happy. He studied really hard, but he still failed the test.

  8 It's the world's oldest mystery. You _____ know the answer.

Workbook page 82 ▶

VOCABULARY
Mysteries

1   **Add the missing vowels to make adjectives related to mysteries.**

  1 __n__xpl__ __n__d

  2 myst__r__ __ __s

  3 __xtr__t__rr__str__ __l

  4 __dd

  5 p__zzl__ng

  6 __l__ __n

  7 s__cr__t

  8 str__ng__

2   **Answer the questions about the words from Exercise 1.**

  1 Which two words mean 'from another world'?

  2 Which word means 'known by very few people'?

3   **Complete the text with adjectives from Exercises 1 and 2.**

I left for school at the usual time, but something seemed wrong. The streets were empty and there was a [1]m_____ feeling in the air. I passed a few people, but they all seemed rather [2]o_____ . I didn't see anyone from school on the way. When I got to school, the gates were closed. Why were they closed? I looked at my watch – 9 am. The gates should be open. This was most [3]p_____ .

I pushed the gates open and walked inside. Where was everyone? Had they been transported away by some [4]e_____ beings and taken to an [5]a_____ planet? Had they all been taken away as part of some [6]s_____ government experiment? What should I do? Run away? No, this was one mystery that couldn't be left [7]u_____ . I had to find out where everyone was.

I opened the school door and walked inside. I saw a man – it was Mr Barns, who looked after the school. I ran up to him.
'Thank goodness!' I cried. 'Where is everyone?'
He gave me a [8]s_____ look.

'At home, probably,' he replied. 'It's Saturday morning.'

Workbook page 84 ▶

LISTENING

1 Match the pictures with the words.

1 fortune-teller   3 housekeeper
2 rope   4 chandelier

2 🔊 2.17 Listen to a story called *The Case of the Mysterious Fall*. Why is the fall mysterious?

3 🔊 2.17 Listen again. Mark the sentences T (true), F (false) or DS (doesn't say).

1 Mr Huntingdon was friendly and sociable.
2 He only spoke to one person each week.
3 He thought of a plan to try and cheat death.
4 Mr Huntingdon tried to call Mrs Crabtree back to the house after she'd left.
5 Mrs Crabtree always started work at 8 am.
6 The fortune-teller's prediction came true.

GRAMMAR
should(n't) have

1 Look at these sentences from the listening. Answer the questions. Then complete the rule.

1 Maybe [Mrs Crabtree] should have asked why.
   a Did Mrs Crabtree ask why?
   b Would it have been a good idea to?
2 He shouldn't have sent Mrs Crabtree home.
   a Did Mr Huntingdon send Mrs Crabtree home?
   b Was it a good idea to?

> **RULE:** To criticise actions in the past, we use *should / shouldn't* + ¹_____ + the ²_____ form of the verb.

2 Write replies to the statements. Use *should have* or *shouldn't have* and suitable verbs. Then practise reading them out in pairs.

0 'I had five slices of pizza! Now I feel sick.'
   'You shouldn't have eaten so much pizza!'
1 'We've broken the TV. Quick! Put the ball away!'
2 'I bought these jeans yesterday, but now I haven't got enough money to buy Dad a birthday present.'
3 'I failed the test!'
4 'Joey didn't invite me to his party.'
5 'You only paid 100 for those tickets? I paid 250!'

3 SPEAKING Work in pairs. Write three sentences about famous people using *should have* or *shouldn't have*. Then read them out without saying the names. Your partner tries to guess who the people are.

Workbook page 82

THiNK VALUES

Thinking carefully before you act

1 SPEAKING Work in pairs. Which do you think was Mr Huntingdon's biggest mistake?

A He should have thought about his plan more carefully.
B He should have told Mrs Crabtree about the fortune-teller's prediction.
C He shouldn't have gone to see the fortune-teller.

2 SPEAKING Look at the pictures. What mistake did each person make? What should they have done?

READING

1 Look at the woman in the photo. Do you know who she is? Why do you think she's famous?

2 Read the article and check your answers.

3 Read the article again. Put the events in the order they happened. Write the numbers in the boxes.

- a The Electra takes off from Miami.
- b Earhart plans to fly around the world.
- c Bones that might be Earhart's are found on a small island.
- d The Electra disappears.
- e Possible evidence of the plane is found.
- f The Electra lands in New Guinea.
- g Earhart flies alone across the Atlantic.
- h The Electra sets off across the Pacific.
- i Earhart tries to find Howland Island.

Lost

Back in 1937, Amelia Earhart was one of the most famous women in the world. She was an author, a fashion designer and a magazine editor, but most of all, she was a pioneering pilot. Five years earlier, at the age of 34, she'd become the first woman to fly solo across the Atlantic Ocean. She also broke many aviation records for going faster and further than any other woman. Every time she landed her plane, she was met by huge crowds wanting to see her and congratulate her. The books that she wrote about her flights were all bestsellers.

That year, Amelia decided she wanted to go one step further. She wanted to go for the ultimate aviation prize and be the first woman to fly around the world. On 1 June, along with her navigator Fred Noonan, Amelia set off from Miami in her plane, a Lockheed Electra, on what would be her biggest – and final – adventure.

The journey was going well when, on 29 June, the pair landed in New Guinea. They'd flown 35,000 km, and they had 11,000 km over the Pacific to go. But on 2 July, while heading towards Howland Island, Amelia and Fred went missing. The next day the world awoke to the news that Amelia Earhart had disappeared into thin air.

Despite a huge search, no sign of the aircraft was ever found. Most people thought that Amelia and Fred must have run out of fuel and that the Electra had gone down in the Pacific Ocean. They couldn't have survived the crash, and they must have died. It seemed the most obvious explanation. But, over the years, other ideas have developed about just what might have happened to the plane.

One theory was that Amelia might have landed her plane on the tiny island of Nikumaroro, not far from Howland Island. In the hope of proving this theory, an expedition went to the island in 2007 to look for signs of the tragic flight. Bones were found that could have been human fingers, but scientists were unable to say for sure if they were. In 2012, another expedition used underwater photography. Images were taken of what could have been an aircraft, but again, investigators couldn't be certain.

Perhaps the most interesting theory is that Earhart disappeared on purpose so that she could spy on the Japanese for the American government. It goes without saying that both countries deny this. But then what else would they say?

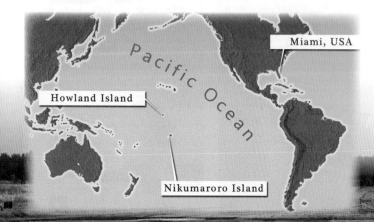

Pacific Ocean

Miami, USA

Howland Island

Nikumaroro Island

GRAMMAR
Modals of deduction (past)

1 **Match 1–3 with a–c. Check your answers in the article on page 88. Then match sentences 1–3 with the rules.**

1 Most people thought that Amelia must have
2 She couldn't have
3 Amelia might have

a survived the crash.
b landed her plane on the island of Nikumaroro.
c run out of fuel.

> **RULE:**
>
> ☐ To say something was *possibly* the case in the past, we use **might** / **could** / **may** + **present perfect**.
>
> ☐ To say something was *definitely not* the case in the past, we use **couldn't** / **can't** + **present perfect**.
>
> ☐ To say something was *definitely* the case in the past, we use **must** + **present perfect**.

2 **Complete the conversation. Use suitable modals and the correct forms of the verbs in brackets.**

'The Case of the Missing Cake'

OLIVER What?! My cake! It's gone!

MATT Really?

OLIVER Yes, it was here an hour ago and now it isn't. Who's taken it?

MATT What about Dad? I heard him saying how hungry he was. In fact, I'm sure it ¹_____ (be) Dad.

OLIVER No, he ²_____ (eat) it. It was chocolate. Dad doesn't like chocolate.

MATT That's true. I suppose Mum ³_____ (take) it. Maybe?

OLIVER No, it ⁴_____ (be) Mum. She's been out all morning.

MATT The dog! He ⁵_____ (jump) onto the table and eaten it. That dog's always doing things like that.

OLIVER Are you mad? The cake was in the fridge. The dog ⁶_____ (got) to it.

MATT Are you sure it wasn't you? I mean, you ⁷_____ (eat) it and forgotten.

OLIVER I'm quite sure it wasn't me. So if it wasn't me, Mum, Dad or the dog, that leaves one person. It ⁸_____ (be) you, Matt!

MATT What?! Me?

OLIVER Yes, and that explains why you've got chocolate all round your mouth!

Workbook page 83 ➤

FUNCTIONS
Making deductions

1 **Read the text and complete the sentences with your opinions. Use *can't*, *must* or *might*.**

In 1998, Russian scientists found a meteorite with a metal screw in it. The rock is at least 300 million years old. At that time, there weren't even any dinosaurs on the planet.

1 It _____ be fake.
2 There _____ have been intelligent life on Earth 300 million years ago.
3 I think someone _____ have made it as a joke.
4 It _____ be from another planet.
5 The scientists _____ have lied about it.

2 **Work in pairs. Discuss your ideas.**

VOCABULARY
Expressions with *go*

1 **Find expressions 1–8 in the text on page 88. Match them with the definitions.**

1 go for
2 go one step further
3 go well
4 … to go
5 go missing
6 go down
7 it goes without saying that
8 go faster

a do something extra
b left / remaining
c disappear
d fall from the sky
e try to achieve
f everyone knows that
g happen as you want
h increase speed

2 **Complete the sentences with the correct forms of the expressions in Exercise 1.**

1 The party's _____ . Everyone's having fun.
2 Four days _____ and then we're on holiday!
3 Police found the child who _____ last week.
4 I want your essay in on Monday and _____ I don't want any excuses.
5 _____ , Dad! The show starts in five minutes.
6 The helicopter _____ over the North Sea.
7 Last week I went swimming twice. This week I want to _____ and go three times.
8 He's training hard. He's _____ the record.

Workbook page 85 ➤

Fiction

1   Read the introduction. What kind of story do you think it is?

2   🔊 2.18   Read and listen to the extract. Check your answer.

How I Met Myself by David A. Hill

One icy winter's evening in Budapest, a man runs straight into John Taylor as he walks home through the narrow streets. John falls over into the snow and looks up at the man's face. 'I felt very afraid. Because what I saw was *me. My* face looking down at me. *My* mouth saying sorry.'

Who is the man, and how will John's life change?

I was walking home from my office one January evening. It was a Monday. The weather was very cold, and there were some low clouds around the tops of buildings. Once I'd left the main road, there weren't many people in the dark, narrow streets of Budapest's Thirteenth District. Everything was very quiet. It felt as if the city was waiting for something.

As I walked I thought about what had happened at work. I had argued with one of the Hungarians I worked with. It was the first serious problem I had had since I'd arrived. I was trying to think what to do about it, and I was also hoping that my wife, Andrea, had made one of her nice, hot soups for dinner.

After about five minutes it started to snow heavily, so that the streets were soon completely white. As I was walking along a very dark part of one street there was the noise of a door shutting loudly inside a building. Then I heard the sound of someone running.

Suddenly, the street door opened and a man came out of it and ran straight into me. I fell over in the snow, shouting something like: 'Hey, watch where you're going!' – my words were loud in the empty street. The man turned to look at me for a moment. 'Sorry,' he said very quietly, in Hungarian, before walking away quickly.

What I saw at that moment, in that dark winter street was very strange, and I felt very afraid. Because what I saw was *me. My* face looking down at me. *My* mouth saying sorry.

[…]

I lay there in the snow for a few moments, trying to understand what had just happened. My first thought was, 'Where has the man gone?' I looked along the street and was just in time to see him turning right at the next corner.

I got up immediately, brushed the snow off my clothes and ran after him. He crossed the road and went into another street. When I got to the corner I saw him going into a doorway. I walked quickly along the empty street, and found it was the entrance to a wine cellar. It was under a block of flats, and you had to go down some steps to get in.

[…]

I stood in the snow for a moment, deciding what to do and looking around me. I had a strange feeling about going down into the wine cellar. I wasn't sure who I'd find there. I looked at my footprints – the dark marks my feet had made in the new snow. My footprints … But only my footprints! Where were his? I looked back along the street. There were only my footprints.

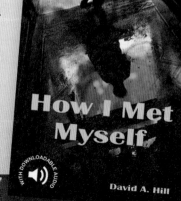

90

3 Read the extract again. Answer the questions.

1 What was the weather like?

2 What was John thinking about on his way home?

3 How did John react to the man in the street?

4 How did the man react?

5 Where did the man go?

6 What was strange about the footprints in the snow?

4 SPEAKING Work in pairs. Discuss these questions.

1 What do you think John finds in the cellar?

2 Who do you think the man is?

WRITING
Explaining a mystery

1 Read the article opposite. Who does the writer think is responsible for the crop circles?

2 Write the underlined expressions in the correct columns.

I'm sure	I'm reasonably sure	I'm not sure

3 The article has three paragraphs. What does the writer talk about in each one?

4 Read about a mystery. Then write three sentences about it. Use a different expression from Exercise 2 in each sentence.

MISSING HELICOPTER

An army helicopter with a pilot, co-pilot and twelve soldiers on board has disappeared off the north coast of Scotland. The last contact with the helicopter was more than twelve hours ago, when the pilot radioed that everything was OK.

No distress signal was received and, despite a huge search over sea and land, no sign of the helicopter has been found. What has happened to army helicopter 487?

5 Write a blog entry (200 words) explaining what you think happened to the missing helicopter.

Mysterious patterns
appear in local field overnight

1 This isn't the first time such a thing has happened and it probably won't be the last time either. For decades, crop circles have been fooling experts, who are still asking, 'What exactly causes these patterns?'

2 Some people say aliens <u>might</u> create this phenomenon. They suggest that aliens come to Earth at night and leave these patterns in our fields. These people are <u>definitely</u> wrong. Even if aliens from other planets existed, how could they land a huge spaceship without anyone noticing? It would be impossible, <u>of course</u>.

3 Humans <u>must have</u> made these crop circles, just as they must have made all the others, but I'm <u>not certain</u> how they did it. <u>Obviously</u>, it <u>can't have</u> been done by just one person; it must have been a group and, <u>more than likely</u>, quite a large one. Also, <u>it's clear</u> that the person, or people, behind the design must be extremely intelligent because these patterns are extraordinarily complex. It was <u>most probably</u> organised by a group of Maths students from a university. It's the kind of thing that students like to do as a joke. But whoever did it, they've <u>certainly</u> got people talking.

READING

1 Look at the photos and answer the questions.

1 Which of the currencies do you recognise? Where are they used?

2 Which one is a digital currency? What do you know about it?

3 Do you think there will still be coins and banknotes in 100 years? Why? / Why not?

2 ◀)) 2.19 Read and listen to the article. Mark the sentences T (true) or F (false).

1 Some people believe the Bitcoin is the future of money. ☐

2 Governments don't take the Bitcoin very seriously. ☐

3 James Howells bought his Bitcoins on the Internet. ☐

4 The value of the Bitcoin greatly increased in its first four years. ☐

5 Howells kept his Bitcoins in an online bank account. ☐

6 There is no chance Howells will ever find his Bitcoin fortune. ☐

▌TRAIN TO THiNK▐

Exaggeration

Sometimes writers exaggerate to create dramatic effect. Of course, this doesn't mean that what they're saying is completely true.

3 Look at these sentences from the article. Which words show that they're exaggerations?

1 Undeniably, the future of money has never been so uncertain.

2 The Internet is by far the most important invention of our lifetime.

4 Read the sentences. Which *isn't* an exaggeration? Underline the words that help you decide.

1 There's no way that Bitcoins will exist in ten years.

2 I found this subject really quite interesting.

3 It's the best article that has ever been written.

5 Rewrite these sentences so they contain an exaggeration.

1 It was a really boring film.

2 Justin Timberlake is a great singer.

3 Brian's good at Maths.

Bitcoins: here to stay?

The Internet is by far and away the most important invention of our lifetime and, over the last 20 years, it's made great changes to our lives. It's changed the way we shop and the way we bank, and now it's making us start to question the way we think about money altogether. Undeniably, the future of money has never been so uncertain. Twenty years from now, will we still be using notes and coins or will we be using something completely different? Many experts predict that soon, different countries won't be paying their bills in their own money any longer. They say that in a few decades' time, everyone all over the world will be using a single currency, the Bitcoin – digital money that has already been called 'the gold of the Internet age' by some.

Up to now, digital money has mostly been the stuff of science fiction films. Recently, however, a number of stories about the Bitcoin have made their way into our newspapers, and governments around the world have started to think about the consequences of such a monetary system. The Bitcoin first made an appearance in 2009, when computer whizz-kids invented 'mining', a way of earning them by solving very complicated mathematical problems.

One such person was James Howells, an IT expert from Newport in Wales. A few years ago, he'd mined Bitcoins worth about £7,500. Like many of the Bitcoin pioneers, he probably didn't think too much about his earnings. That was until, one day in 2013, he discovered that the value of his Bitcoins had gone up and they were now worth about £4 million!

So where had Howells stored his treasure? After looking for a long time – on the hard disk of his computer, on every single USB stick he could find in his home, and on various CDs

he had lying around in his study – the terrible truth slowly dawned on him. He'd stored the Bitcoins on an old hard disk, and he'd thrown it away while clearing out old computer stuff the previous summer. Howells rushed to the recycling centre he'd taken it to. He was told he'd have to search though waste more than a metre deep in an area the size of a football field.

Howells has told the Internet community the location of the recycling centre and has promised a reward to anyone who finds the treasure. Theoretically, if the hard disk hasn't been smashed, someone might find it one day, and it might still contain the data. Computer hard disks are pretty tough and can keep data even when they're underwater for quite some time. But the chances are still small. The recycling centre uses big magnets to sort out the waste, and magnets can erase data. Even if someone did come across the hard disk, there might not be a trace of Howells' Bitcoins on it any more!

SPEAKING

Work in pairs. Discuss these questions.

1 How would you feel if you were James Howells?
2 Have you ever lost important data? What happened?
3 Do you think the Bitcoin is here to stay?

GRAMMAR
Future continuous

1 **Complete the sentences from the article on page 93. Then (circle) the correct words to complete the rule.**

   1 Twenty years from now, will _____ still _____ notes and coins?

   2 In a few decades' time, everyone all over the world _____ a single currency.

> **RULE:** We use the **future continuous** to talk about things that will be in progress at *a specified / an unspecified* time in the future.

2 **Complete the sentences with the correct forms of the verbs.**

   1 Tomorrow at 10 o'clock, I _____ (sit) on a train.

   2 Lucky you! This time next week, you _____ (enjoy) your holidays.

   3 Susan is still at university, but a year from now, she _____ (work) in her dad's company.

   4 What _____ I _____ (do) three years from now? I have no idea.

   5 Talk to James now. Tonight he _____ (play) tennis, so you won't be able to reach him.

   6 Tomorrow afternoon, we _____ (have) a drink in a café next to the river.

3 **Complete the text. Use the future simple or future continuous form of the verbs.**

not travel | drink | wake up | put on
not work | pay | lie | have

I know where I'll be ten years from now. I [1]_____ 50 hours a week in a small office. I [2]_____ two hours every day to get to and from work. No, I [3]_____ on a beautiful Caribbean beach! I [4]_____ coconut water and reading a good book. Every day will be the same. I [5]_____ late and I [6]_____ a long, lazy breakfast. I [7]_____ my shorts and walk down to the beach to meet my friends. And how [8]_____ I _____ for all of this? I'm going to find James Howells' computer!

4 **SPEAKING Work in pairs. Discuss what you will be doing at these times.**

   1 an hour from now   3 this time next week

   2 at 8 o'clock tonight   4 on 1 January

> *An hour from now, I'll be having lunch.*

Workbook page 90

VOCABULARY
Money and value

1 **Match the words with the definitions.**

a tip | £(X) off | a reward | a bargain | to owe
a refund | be worth | not good value for money
valuable | on offer

   1 money that you get for doing something helpful (for example, finding something that was lost)

   2 money that's paid back to you (for example, if you return something to a shop)

   3 extra money to thank someone (for example, a waiter) for a service

   4 to need to pay someone

   5 available at a good price (usually for a short time)

   6 money taken away from the original price

   7 something you get at a really good price

   8 not worth its price

   9 having a very high value

  10 have a value of

2 **Complete the sentences with the words from Exercise 1.**

   0 I'm not buying the shoes in this shop. There's another one nearby where they're *on offer* .

   1 I _____ Kylie £20. I mustn't forget to repay her.

   2 Mr Brown offered a big _____ for any information that would help him to find his dog.

   3 The taxi driver was very helpful, so we gave him a good _____ .

   4 Have a look at this old coin. Do you think it's _____ much?

   5 I bought this expensive laptop last week. Today I saw it in the shop for £100 _____ .

   6 The tablet didn't work, so I took it back to the shop and they gave me a _____ .

   7 I paid £50 for this toy and it broke after a week. It really was _____ .

   8 I waited until after Christmas and got the bike for half price. It was a real _____ .

   9 This vase is 3,000 years old and very _____ .

3 **SPEAKING Work in pairs. Discuss the questions.**

   1 What's the most valuable thing that teenagers usually own?

   2 What are some good ways to get a bargain?

   3 In what situations might you give someone a reward or a tip? Have you ever received one?

   4 Have you ever had to ask for a refund? What for?

Workbook page 92

MONEY – would you believe it?!

1 The oldest type of money (and also the shape of the first bronze coins) was …
- **A** bananas.
- **B** shells.
- **C** cows.
- **D** trees.

3 All the banknotes ever produced for the board game Monopoly would create a tower that is …
- **A** 10 km high.
- **B** 100 km high.
- **C** 200 km high.
- **D** 2,000 km high.

5 An American named Mueller once paid $10,000 for a …
- **A** piece of chewed gum.
- **B** pair of jeans.
- **C** bowl of chicken soup.
- **D** used toothbrush.

2 Some special cash machines in Japan give out money that is …
- **A** calorie-free.
- **B** bacteria-free.
- **C** sugar-free.
- **D** paper-free.

4 Imagine you had 10 billion banknotes (of any currency). If you spent one banknote every second, your money would last for …
- **A** 3 years.
- **B** 31 years.
- **C** 317 years.
- **D** 3,178 years.

LISTENING

1 Look at the questionnaire and try to guess the answers. Then compare with a partner.

2 **◀))2.20** Listen to an extract from the quiz show *Show Me The Money!* Check your answers.

▌THiNK SELF-ESTEEM ▌▌▌▌▌

What's important for your future?

1 Choose the statement that you agree with most.

1 Twenty years from now, I hope I'll have enough money to buy …
- **A** everything I want.
- **B** everything I need.

2 It's important to have a job that …
- **A** you enjoy.
- **B** pays a lot of money.

3 When I look into the future, I can see …
- **A** a time when I won't need to learn anything any more.
- **B** that I'll always be learning new things.

2 **SPEAKING** Work in pairs. Compare your answers.

3 Match the types of goal with the statements in Exercise 1.
- a financial goals
- b educational goals
- c professional goals

4 Write sentences about your goals. Write about at least one goal in each of the areas in Exercise 3.

When I'm 60, I'll be learning to play the guitar.
In 20 years, I'll be working as a translator and I'll be able to speak four languages.
When I'm 50, I won't need to work any more.

Pronunciation

Short and long vowel sounds: /ɪ/ – /iː/ and /ɒ/ – /əʊ/
Go to page 121.

READING

1 Look at the people in the photos. If Nigel Wood, a nurse, earns £30,000 a year, how much do you think the other two get?

2 Read the web forum page and check your answers.

3 Read the forum entries again.
✳ Answer the questions.

Who thinks that footballers' high salaries …

1 cause problems for other teams?
2 might cause people problems in the future?
3 need to be looked at seriously by the authorities?
4 are a good thing?
5 are bad for young people's education?
6 are a question of economics?

Wayne Rooney: football player for Manchester United

Debbie Helps: senior manager in an international company

Nigel Wood: nurse with 10 years' experience

ARE THEY WORTH IT?

Wayne Rooney's contract with Manchester United sees him earning a reported £15.6 million a year. This makes him the highest-paid player in the English Premier League … for now. It means that by the end of his five-year contract, he'll have earned more than £70 million for playing football. And that isn't counting the money he'll get from sponsorship deals.

Of course, Rooney isn't the only one. In fact, Premiership footballers earn on average £1.1 million a year. That's 14 times more than the average person working in management and an incredible 36 times more than someone working in public service, such as a nurse or a teacher. As the footballers turn up to matches in their Ferraris and Aston Martins, their fans take the bus or walk. The question we're asking is: are these players really worth the money?

In a word, no. The problem with the current system is that it sets such a bad example for the younger generation. So many teenage boys want to be footballers or pop stars because they see it as a quick way to make a lot of money. They don't think about the fact that for every boy who makes it, there are thousands who don't. Of course, they won't have thought about that before they leave school and then it'll be too late.
UKmum

The Football Assocation (FA) keeps saying they want to control the amount of money a footballer can earn, which will be a good thing. However, the FA is never the quickest organisation at getting things done. Who knows, hopefully by the year 2050, they'll have sorted this mess out. Something needs to be done.
Lucy88

The top footballers make far more money for their clubs than they get paid in salaries. These clubs make a fortune from the sales of tickets, TV rights and football shirts because of these stars. It's a question of business and these players are good for business. Of course they deserve their salaries.
Simonsays

The problem with the current situation is that only the really big clubs can afford to pay these kinds of salaries, so they get all the best players and win everything. This means they get more money from sponsorship and TV and they can increase their players' salaries even more. It makes life really difficult for the smaller clubs.
Jimmy

GRAMMAR
Future perfect

1 **Complete the sentences from the forum entries on page 96. Then read the rule and complete it with the words.**

1 By the end of his five-year contract, he _____ more than £70 million for playing football.

2 Of course, they _____ about that before they leave school and then it'll be too late.

3 Who knows, hopefully by the year 2050, _____ this mess out.

have | past participle | will

> **RULE:** We use the **future perfect** to talk about actions that will finish at some time between now and a specified time in the future.
>
>
>
> now   the end of the year
>
> £1 million   £2 million   £3 million
>
> *By the end of the year, he'll have earned more than £3 million.*
>
> ● We form it with ¹_____ + ²_____ + ³_____ .
> ● We often use it with *by* + a point in time or *by the time* + a time clause.
>   *By 2050, ...*
>   *By the time I'm 50, ...*

2 **Complete the sentences with the future perfect form of the verbs.**

1 The government _____ (build) lots of new houses here by 2030.

2 By the time I'm 35, I _____ (work) in IT for over ten years.

3 If I work really hard, I _____ (do) my homework by the time the match starts on TV.

4 The test is from 9 to 12 tomorrow morning. So at 10 o'clock, I _____ (not finish) it.

5 By that time, I _____ (buy) my first house.

6 I hope that three years from now, I _____ (visit) one or two other countries.

3 **SPEAKING** **Work in pairs. Look at the questions and make notes. Then compare your ideas.**

1 Which tasks will / won't you have finished by 6 pm tomorrow?

2 What will / won't you have done by the end of the year?

3 Which goals will / won't you have achieved six years from now?

Workbook page 90

VOCABULARY
Jobs and work

1 **Match the words with the definitions.**

public service | education | healthcare | law
management | finance | salary | qualifications
employer | employee

1 abilities or experience needed for a particular job

2 jobs paid for by the government

3 people who make the big decisions in a company

4 teaching and learning

5 a person or organisation that people work for

6 an area of work related to managing money

7 the money a person is paid for doing a job

8 an area of work related to the legal system

9 an area of work related to medicine

10 someone who's paid to work for someone else

2 **Complete the sentences with words from Exercise 1.**

1 Her dad works in _____ . He's a nurse.

2 Margaret Bourne is the director of _____ for a big company. She decides on all the investments.

3 Joanna was a police officer and now she's a teacher. She's been in _____ all her professional life.

4 Larry is a teacher. He works in _____ .

5 The company suffered years of bad _____ .

6 Microsoft is the biggest _____ in the Seattle area.

7 A degree and some experience in IT are necessary _____ for this job.

8 James works in _____ . He's a judge.

9 Allan got a new job with a higher _____ .

10 She's been an _____ of this company for 25 years.

3 **SPEAKING** **Work in pairs. Discuss these questions.**

1 Which of the areas of work in Exercise 1 would you be most / least interested in? Why?

2 Would you rather be an employer or an employee? Why?

Workbook page 92

WRITING
My life in the future

Write about your life 30 years from now (150–200 words). Think about the things that you:

● will be doing.
● will have done.
● won't have done.
● will still want to do.

Strapped for cash

1 **Look at the photos and answer the questions.**

What has Jeff found?

Why do you think they're looking at the woman?

2 ◀))2.23 **Now read and listen to the photostory. Check your answers.**

LEO I'd really like one of these fancy desserts. Like this one, with nuts and everything, and the banana …

FLORA A banana split! Mmm, they're amazing. Let's see. Oh, they're £6.99. I don't have that kind of money.

MIA Tell me about it. I'd really like one of those hot chocolate drinks with all the extras. But I just can't afford it.

LEO Well, don't look at me. I'm broke too. No banana splits for me either, I'm afraid.
(Jeff arrives)

JEFF Hi, you lot. Wow, you don't look very happy.

MIA Just feeling sorry for ourselves. We're all strapped for cash, same as usual.

JEFF Ah, well, in that case, you should be *really* happy to see me!

LEO And why's that, Jeff?

JEFF Look what I found! Outside here, on the street, by the shoe shop. My lucky day, eh? And your lucky day, too! Let's go crazy – desserts are on me!

MIA But, Jeff, the money isn't ours. We can't just spend it on ourselves like that.

JEFF Why not? There's no way to find the person who lost it, is there?

MIA I'm just saying it doesn't feel right, that's all.

JEFF Don't be silly. Come on, order whatever you want.

LEO OK. If you say so, Jeff!

WAITRESS The usual, Mrs Brady? A large coffee?

MRS BRADY I'd better have a small coffee today. You know, this morning I lost £20.

WAITRESS Oh no! That's a shame. I'm really sorry to hear that.

MRS BRADY Yes. I must have lost it around here somewhere. That's a lot of money for me.

WAITRESS Oh dear! What a pity! Never mind – maybe you just misplaced it and you'll find it again.

MIA Did you hear that? We ate the old lady's money!

FLORA I know. How awful!

LEO Look what you did, Jeff!

JEFF Don't look at me! It's not my fault. I didn't eat all of this by myself, you know!

DEVELOPING SPEAKING

3 Work in pairs. Discuss what happens next in the story. Write down your ideas.

We think they go and speak to the old lady and give her some money.

4 ▶️ **EP4** Watch and find out how the story continues.

5 Match 1–7 with a–g.

1 The four friends decide ☐
2 Jeff ☐
3 Flora ☐
4 Leo ☐
5 Mia ☐
6 In the café, Flora ☐
7 The old lady ☐

a gets some money in advance for a job.
b gets money from a jar at home.
c gives some money to the old lady.
d to get money to give to the old lady.
e finds some more money in her pocket.
f sells some old books.
g finds money in all kinds of different places.

PHRASES FOR FLUENCY

1 Find these expressions in the photostory. Who says them? How do you say them in your language?

1 same as usual
2 Don't look at me!
3 Hi, you lot.
4 … is / are on me.
5 … , that's all.
6 It's not my fault!

2 Use the expressions in Exercise 1 to complete the conversations.

1 A I haven't got enough money for lunch.
 B Well, _____! I can't pay.
 C It's OK. I'll pay for the food. Lunch _____!

2 A _____ . How are you all?
 B Oh, _____ , really. Nothing changes a lot, does it?

3 A Wow, this room is really untidy!
 B Hey! _____! Julie made the mess, not me.
 C OK, calm down. I didn't say it was you. I just said it was untidy, _____ .

WordWise
by

1 What do the phrases in bold refer to? Match 1–4 with a–d.

1 It's called 'the gold of the Internet age' **by some people**.
2 He got the Bitcoins **by solving** complicated Maths problems.
3 I found it in the street, **by the shoe shop**.
4 Dad, I need £20 **by tomorrow**.

a a location
b a time in the future
c a way to do something
d the person / people who do something

2 Complete the sentences with the phrases.

by the entrance | by the end of class
by the football club | by selling

1 Please finish Exercise 2 _____ .
2 He's paid a lot _____ that he plays for.
3 Meet me tomorrow _____ to the cinema.
4 Jeff got money _____ old books.

Workbook page 92 ➡️

FUNCTIONS
Sympathising

1 Look back at the photostory. Complete the extracts with the phrases in the list.

That's a shame | Never mind | How awful
What a pity | I'm really sorry

MRS BRADY This morning I lost £20.
WAITRESS Oh no! [1]_____! [2]_____ to hear that.
MRS BRADY [...] That's a lot of money for me.
WAITRESS Oh dear! [3]_____! [4]_____ – maybe you just misplaced it and you'll find it again.

MIA We ate the old lady's money!
FLORA I know. [5]_____!

2 Work in pairs. Write four-line conversations like the one in Exercise 1 about each of these situations. Then act them out.

You tell your friend that …
- your exam results are very bad.
- you lost some money.
- you broke your mobile phone.

THiNK EXAMS

LISTENING
Part 2: Sentence completion

Workbook page 89

1 **◀))2.24** You will hear Conner talking about the Royal Mint, where money is made. For questions 1–10, complete the sentences with 1–3 words.

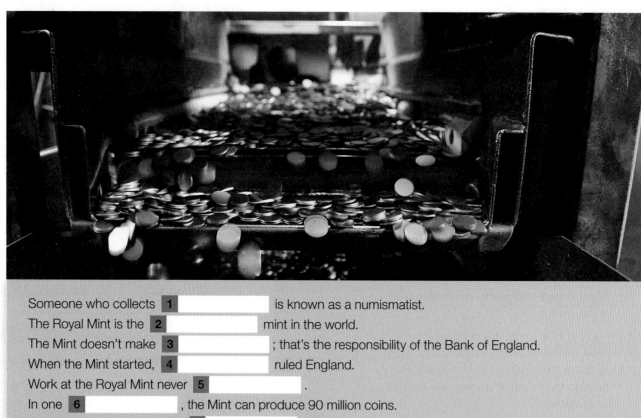

Someone who collects **1** [_____] is known as a numismatist.

The Royal Mint is the **2** [_____] mint in the world.

The Mint doesn't make **3** [_____] ; that's the responsibility of the Bank of England.

When the Mint started, **4** [_____] ruled England.

Work at the Royal Mint never **5** [_____] .

In one **6** [_____] , the Mint can produce 90 million coins.

The Mint produces coins for **7** [_____] different nations as well as the UK.

A metal disc with nothing printed on it is called a **8** [_____] .

In 2012, the Mint made coins to commemorate the **9** [_____] and the Queen's Diamond Jubilee.

Because of security concerns, you can't **10** [_____] the Royal Mint.

WRITING
Part 1: Essay

Workbook page 97

2 In your English class, you have been talking about money. Now your English teacher has asked you to write an essay for homework.

Write your essay using all the notes and giving reasons for your point of view. Give your opinion (for or against) in the last paragraph.

Is it more important to enjoy your job or earn a lot of money?

Notes – Write about:

1 material possessions.

2 happiness and job satisfaction.

3 _____ (your own idea)

Write your essay in 140–190 words.

VOCABULARY

1 Complete the sentences with the words / phrases in the list. There are four extra words / phrases.

unexplained | went missing | bargain | mysterious | worth | employer | on offer
employee | alien | refund | go very well | salary | owe | going for

1 He's worked for that company for 25 years now. He's their oldest _____ .
2 Nobody knows what happened to him. The mystery of his disappearance is still _____ .
3 His plane _____ over the Atlantic Ocean.
4 Michael lent me some money last month. I still _____ him 75p.
5 I bought this camera for half price. It was a real _____!
6 You've paid too much for it. It isn't _____ that much money.
7 I'm afraid the exam didn't _____ . I'm sure I've failed it.
8 He's been training all year. He's _____ a gold medal.
9 You know those trainers you like? They're _____ at the moment! You should buy them.
10 It's broken. I think you should take it back and ask for a _____ .

/10

GRAMMAR

2 Complete the sentences with the verbs in the list. There are two extra verbs.

might | must have | should have | won't be working | might have
will be living | will have written | couldn't have

1 She hurt her head when she fell off her scooter. She _____ worn a helmet.
2 She's a really good player. If she'd entered the race, she _____ won it.
3 By the time I'm 25, I _____ on a Greek island!
4 In ten years' time, I _____ for anybody. I'll have my own company.
5 He _____ stopped the accident. He was too late.
6 By the time I'm thirty, I _____ my first novel.

3 Find and correct the mistake in each sentence.

1 He shouldn't has left the window open. That's how the burglar got in.
2 She might like the film if she had come.
3 In ten years' time, I hope I will have working in London.
4 Where will you living in 20 years' time?
5 He must be finished his homework by now.
6 In five years' time, I will have climb Mount Everest.

/12

FUNCTIONAL LANGUAGE

4 Circle the correct words.

1 A No way! This piece of rock *can't / mustn't* be from another planet.
  B I don't agree with you. I think it *can / might* be.
2 A I'm *many / really* sorry I can't come to the football match with you.
  B Never *mind / know*. You can come with me next week.
3 A Hi, you *lots / lot*. I'm sorry I'm late. What would you like to eat?
  B Same as *normal / usual*, please!
4 A It goes without *seeing / saying* that Peter can't come on Saturday.
     He crashed his scooter.
  B How *shameful / awful*!

/8

MY SCORE	/30
22 – 30	
10 – 21	
0 – 9	

HELP!

READING

1 Look at the photos. What is the same about all of them? What is different in each one?

2 Read the sentences. Which photo(s) might each one refer to?

   1 It took the rescuers a long time to bring the victim down.

   2 The victim was given first aid before going to hospital.

   3 The helicopter emergency services managed to pull the victim out of the sea.

   4 After the rescue operation, the victim was taken to hospital for treatment.

3 Make a list of people and things that can help in an emergency. Compare your ideas with others in the class.

Things	People
ambulance	police officer

4 Look at the photos on page 103 and the title of the news report. What do you think it's about? Read the report quickly and check your ideas.

5 ◀)) 2.25 Read the report again and listen. Mark the sentences T (true) or F (false).

   1 The accident happened on a windy day. ☐

   2 A mother and her baby were swimming in the sea. ☐

   3 Mr Reeder thought for a long time before he went into the water. ☐

   4 The baby was in the water for about five minutes. ☐

   5 The person who helped the baby breathe again was a nurse. ☐

   6 Mr Reeder knew the baby was OK when he saw the nurse. ☐

   7 Mr Reeder was happy when the boy's grandfather told him the news. ☐

   8 Mr Reeder agrees that he was brave that day. ☐

A

B

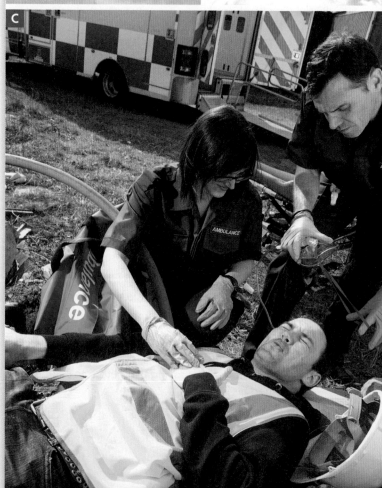

C

LOCAL MAN'S BRAVERY REWARDED

George Reeder, 63, of Watchet in Somerset has been given a bravery certificate for saving the life of a six-month-old baby.

It was a cold and windy morning in Watchet in January 2013. The local harbour master, George Reeder, was carrying out his regular duties when he heard a noise that caught his attention. On the other side of the harbour, some people were pointing and shouting, so he cycled over as fast as he could.

Mr Reeder expected to see a dog in the sea, but instead he saw a baby's buggy in about four metres of freezing cold water. A woman was screaming desperately – her six-month-old baby boy was strapped into the buggy and was in the water. The strong wind had blown the buggy into the sea. Mr Reeder quickly decided to do something.

'I went over and saw that the buggy was upside-down … and I jumped in,' said Mr Reeder. He pulled the buggy over to the sea wall. Some other people helped to tie a rope to the buggy, and they managed to pull it out of the water and to safety, but not before the baby had spent around five minutes in the sea.

Tanya Allen, a passer-by (who, fortunately, was a nurse), gave the baby CPR and was able to get him to breathe again. Mr Reeder remembered seeing a little bit of breath coming out of the baby's mouth. 'I thought, he's all right. He's alive. Brilliant!' he said. Then an air ambulance helicopter arrived and the baby was taken to hospital. Mr Reeder said it was incredible that the baby survived. 'It's such a miracle,' Mr Reeder added.

After he'd finished helping the baby and the helicopter had gone, Mr Reeder went home to recover from the experience. The child's grandfather knew Mr Reeder and, a little later, went to his house to tell him that the boy was out of danger. Mr Reeder was very relieved and happy to hear that.

Mr Reeder said that he hadn't really been brave. 'It was everyone – from Tanya doing the CPR to the helicopter pilot,' he said. 'I'm just glad I could help.' But when Mr Reeder got the certificate, a council spokesperson said that what he'd done was very courageous. 'This was an extremely brave act, as he put his own life at risk.' The council has advised local people to avoid walking along the seafront in very windy weather.

■ TRAIN TO THiNK ■

Understanding cause and effect

There is only a cause-and-effect relationship between two ideas if we can prove that one thing leads to another.

6 Match causes 1–5 with effects a–e. Then check your answers in the article.

1 The baby was in great danger. ☐
2 He saved the baby's life. ☐
3 He heard a noise. ☐
4 He learned that the baby was OK. ☐
5 The baby wasn't breathing. ☐

a He got a bravery certificate.
b He cycled quickly to see what was happening.
c A nurse gave first aid.
d He jumped in the water without thinking.
e He felt very relieved.

7 Complete 1–3 with a cause or an effect.

1 The wind became very strong, so the helicopter …
2 … , so we decided to call the emergency services.
3 … Therefore, the victim was taken to hospital.

SPEAKING

Work in pairs. Discuss these questions.

1 Mr Reeder said he hadn't been brave. Do you agree with him? Why (not)?
2 Do you think that you could do the same thing in Mr Reeder's situation?
3 Do you know any other stories of ordinary people being heroes?

GRAMMAR
Verbs followed by gerund or infinitive

1 Complete the sentences from the news report on page 103. What do the verbs have in common?

1 Mr Reeder remembered _____ a little bit of breath coming out of the baby's mouth.

2 After he'd finished _____ the baby and the helicopter had gone, Mr Reeder went home.

3 The council has advised local people to avoid _____ along the seafront in very windy weather.

2 Now complete these sentences from the report. What do these verbs have in common? Then complete the rule. Label the columns with *to + infinitive* or *gerund*.

1 He expected _____ a dog in the sea.

2 Mr Reeder quickly decided _____ something.

3 Some other people helped _____ a rope to the buggy.

4 They managed _____ it out of the water.

RULE:

Followed by [1]_____	Followed by [2]_____
enjoy, (don't) mind, (can't) stand, finish, imagine, feel like, suggest, practise, miss, avoid	hope, promise, learn, expect, decide, afford, offer, choose, want
---

3 Complete the sentences. Use a verb from A followed by a verb from B in each sentence.

A ~~choose~~ | hope | avoid | feel like | decide | finish

B ~~stay~~ | watch | see | buy | speak | go

0 I can't believe you _chose to stay_ at home last night rather than come to the cinema with us.

1 After a lot of thought, I _____ a new bike.

2 Bye! I _____ you again soon.

3 I'm so tired. I just _____ to bed.

4 I really don't like him, so I _____ to him.

5 I'll help you. I'll just _____ this video first.

Workbook page 100

Pronunciation
Strong and weak forms: /tuː/ and /tə/
Go to page 121.

VOCABULARY
Danger and safety

1 Replace the <u>underlined</u> phrases with the words and phrases in the list.

rescued | dangerous | in danger | to safety
survived | recover | save his life | out of danger

1 He was in a terrible accident, but he <u>didn't die</u>.

2 Don't go into that room! There might be something <u>that could hurt you</u> in there.

3 She went to hospital to <u>get better</u>.

4 Mr Reeder <u>took</u> the baby <u>away from a bad situation</u>.

5 He managed to <u>stop him being killed</u>.

6 People who lived near the volcano moved away so they were <u>not going to be harmed</u>.

7 People who drive really fast sometimes put their lives <u>in a situation of potential harm</u>.

8 The helicopter took him <u>to a place where he wasn't going to be harmed</u>.

2 (Circle) the correct words.

1 Thank you so much – you *rescued / saved* my life!

2 We can go in here. It isn't *safe / dangerous* at all.

3 We were lucky to *survive / save* the accident.

4 The boat sank, but all the passengers were *recovered / rescued* by another boat.

5 Fortunately, he *recovered / saved* from his injuries.

6 No one died. All the passengers *rescued / survived*.

7 She was badly hurt in the accident, but fortunately she's *in / out of* danger now.

8 The helicopter flew the survivors *in danger / to safety*.

3 **SPEAKING** Work in pairs or small groups. Discuss these questions.

1 In which sports and activities are people in danger? Do you do them? Would you like to? Why (not)?

2 Do you know of someone who has been in a bad accident and survived? How did he/she survive?

3 Do you know anyone who's saved another person's life? Who was it? What happened?

Workbook page 102

LISTENING

1 In which picture(s) can you see these things?

a well | a farmer | a donkey | a wheelbarrow | earth

2 ◀))2.28 You're going to hear a story about a farmer, a donkey and a well. Put the pictures in the order you think tells the story. Then listen and check.

3 ◀))2.28 Listen again. Answer the questions.

1 Why didn't the farmer throw a rope to the donkey?
2 Why didn't the farmer go into the well?
3 Why did the farmer throw earth in the well?
4 Why did the donkey stop making a noise?
5 What does the presenter think the moral is?

4 **SPEAKING** Work in pairs or small groups. What do you think the moral of the story is? Do you know any other stories with morals?

GRAMMAR
to / in order to / so as to

1 Look at the sentences from the listening. Then complete the rule.

1 The farmer ran over **to** see what had happened.
2 He couldn't throw a rope down **in order to** pull the donkey out.
3 I'm doing this **so as to** help the donkey die quickly.

> **RULE:** We can use *to* + **infinitive** to talk about purpose. In more formal language or in writing, we can also use _____ or _____ + **infinitive**.

2 Think about the stories in the unit so far. Match 1–4 with a–d. Then rewrite each pair as one sentence using the words in brackets.

0 Why did the farmer get some earth?   *e*
   The farmer got some earth to bury the donkey.
1 Why did Mr Reeder jump into the water?
2 Why did the farmer look into the well?
3 Why did the nurse stop on the seafront?
4 Why do the authorities say not to walk on the seafront in windy weather?

a rescue a small boy. (to)
b prevent future accidents. (in order to)
c see why the donkey was quiet. (so as to)
d help the baby boy. (in order to)
e ~~bury the donkey.~~ (to)

Workbook page 100 ▶

FUNCTIONS
Expressing purpose

1 Match 1–5 with a–e.

1 Why did she send you a card?
2 Why did you get up early yesterday?
3 Why did you go into town?
4 Why did he save his money for so long?
5 Why did they move house?

a To watch the sun come up.
b In order to get a new guitar.
c So as to have more room.
d To get a present for my mum.
e To say thank you.

2 Work in pairs. Think of three *Why do / did you ... ?* questions to ask your partner. Ask and answer each other's questions.

▮ THiNK SELF-ESTEEM ▮

Offering and accepting help

1 Mark each statement from 1 to 5 (1 = I strongly agree; 5 = I strongly disagree).

1 Helping someone else makes me feel good.
2 I only help someone when they ask me to.
3 You can always help another person.
4 I only help people when I think they can also help me.
5 I try to do something myself before I ask for help.

2 **SPEAKING** Discuss your answers in small groups.

READING

1 In the UK, you dial 999 for the emergency services. What number do you call in your country? Does it depend on the type of emergency?

2 Read the article. Which of the 'emergency' calls do pictures A–C show?

EMERGENCY? WHAT EMERGENCY?

An emergency service should be exactly that: a service that you phone in an emergency. You might need to call an ambulance if you're in a car accident or the police if you see a crime happening. But some people phone the emergency services for such unimportant reasons that it's hard to believe these calls are real. Then again, there are some crazy people out there, so perhaps it isn't really so surprising that the emergency services get some unusual calls.

Here are some examples that we've heard about from emergency centres all over the world.

1 'I ordered food from a Chinese takeaway and it hasn't come yet. I'm so hungry! Can you tell them to hurry up, please?'

2 'My children are making such a loud noise upstairs that I can't think properly. Can you come and calm them down, please?'

3 'My car's parked outside my house. There's a lot of snow on the road. I'm too scared to go out to my car.'

4 'My brother-in-law has been staying with us for two weeks. He's so boring that I can't stand it any more. Please come and tell him to go home.'

5 'There's a black cat in my garden. Black cats are such unlucky animals. Can someone please come and take it away?'

6 'There's a big bright thing in the sky. I'm really worried. I want someone to come and look, please.' (A police car went. It was the moon.)

7 'I'm trying to find a shop in the town centre and I can't. I'm so tired that I'm almost in tears.'

8 'I think the Prime Minister is such a good-looking man, and I want to phone him and tell him. Can you give me his telephone number, please?'

These calls are amusing to read about, but they can have very serious consequences. 'Every call takes about a minute,' said one man who works in emergency services. 'Perhaps that doesn't sound a very long time, but in that one minute, other people are calling who really have an emergency. And for them, a minute might be really important.'

So let's get really serious: please THINK before you call the emergency services. And, of course, remember that you should never phone them with information that's untrue – it's irresponsible and it's also illegal.

3 Read the first and last paragraphs again. Answer the questions.

1 What examples are given of real emergencies?

2 Why should you never phone emergency services with untrue information?

4 **SPEAKING** Work in small groups. Which of the calls do you think was the craziest?

GRAMMAR
so and *such*

1 Complete the sentences from the article on page 106. Then complete the rule.

1 I'm _____ hungry. Can you tell them to hurry up, please?
2 I think the Prime Minister is _____ a good-looking man.
3 Black cats are _____ unlucky animals.

> **RULE:** We can use *so* or *such* to emphasise adjectives, adverbs, nouns and noun phrases:
> 1 _____ + adjective / adverb
> 2 _____ (+ *a* / *an*) (+ adjective) + noun

2 Now complete these sentences from the article and complete the rule.

1 He's _____ that I can't stand it any more.
2 I'm _____ that I'm almost in tears.
3 My children are making _____ that I can't think properly.
4 Some people call 999 for _____ that it's hard to believe these calls are real.

> **RULE:** We also use *so* or *such* to show how one thing is a result of another. We form the sentence in the same way and *so* or *such* is followed by _____ .

3 Join the pairs of sentences. Use *so / such ... that.*

0 We were very late. We had to take a taxi.
We were so late that we had to take a taxi.
1 It was a very bad accident. Two people had to go to hospital.
2 It was very windy. It was dangerous to walk there.
3 The well was deep. The donkey couldn't get out.
4 The road was very icy. It was dangerous to drive on it.
5 They were careless people. They always forgot to lock the door to their house.

> Workbook page 101

VOCABULARY
Adjectives with negative prefixes

1 Replace the underlined words with one word.

0 Mr Reeder was <u>not concerned</u> about his own safety.
unconcerned
1 It was <u>not possible</u> to get the donkey out of the well.
2 The farmer thought that the donkey was dead and he was <u>not happy</u>.
3 It's <u>not surprising</u> that they get so many crazy calls.
4 Some people call 999 for <u>not important</u> reasons.
5 These <u>not necessary</u> calls take up a lot of time.
6 You should never phone with information that's <u>not true</u> – it's <u>not responsible</u> and it's also <u>not legal</u>.

2 Which negative prefixes do these adjectives take? Write them in the correct columns.

~~surprising~~ | comfortable | formal | patient responsible | logical | possible | helpful polite | regular | legal | expensive | healthy concerned | afraid

un–	im–	in–	ir–	il–
unsurprising				

3 Complete the questions. Use adjectives from Exercise 2 with negative prefixes.

0 Do you think it's very *impolite* to talk with food in your mouth?
1 Do you think it's _____ to eat fried food?
2 Do you worry about exams, or are you _____?
3 Do you sometimes get a little _____ when you have to wait for things?
4 Do your parents think you're too _____ to be at home alone all weekend?
5 Do you think that _____ clothes are always bad quality?

4 **SPEAKING** Work in pairs. Discuss the questions in Exercise 3.

> Workbook page 102

107

Culture

1 Look at the photos. What do you think these men escaped from? How do you think they did it?

2 🔊 2.29 Read and listen to the article. Check your answers.

THE GREAT ESCAPE

After many tragedies, there are always stories of people who have shown an amazing ability to survive. Here are two stories which remind us that miracles can happen.

On 5 August, 2010, the San José copper and gold mine in the Atacama Desert in Chile collapsed and 33 miners were trapped underground. The mine had a poor safety record, and there were fears that the missing men wouldn't come out alive. A rescue team immediately began drilling into the ground where it was thought the men might be. On Day 17, when the drill was brought out of the ground, there was a note taped to it. In bright red letters it read: 'We are alive and well in the shelter, all 33 of us.' It was the news the whole country had been waiting for and the Chilean government promised to bring them out alive. For the next seven weeks, rescue teams from all over the world worked together to drill a hole big enough to bring out the men, who were waiting 700 metres below the ground. It was a long, difficult and dangerous job, but on 13 October, more than a billion people around the world watched live on TV as the first of the miners was finally brought above ground. Twenty-four hours later, the last miner, number 33, was reunited with his family and friends.

B

In June 2013, a rescue diver was swimming through the wreck of the tugboat *Jascon-4* when he got an enormous shock: a hand reached out and grabbed his leg. The ship had sunk two and a half days earlier and was now lying 30 metres below the surface of the water. The diver, who was part of a team looking for the bodies of the 13 crew members, hadn't expected to find anyone alive. But one man had managed to survive. Twenty-nine-year-old Harrison Okene from Nigeria was the ship's cook. When the ship got into trouble in rough seas and started turning over, Okene found an air pocket and put his head in it. As the ship sank towards the sea floor, he expected the pocket to fill with water, but it didn't. Despite the freezing water and having nothing to eat or drink, Okene had enough air to breathe. There was nothing he could do except wait. Sixty hours after the ship went down, Okene heard knocking and knew that rescue teams had entered the ship. He still wasn't safe, and a complicated plan was needed to bring him slowly to the surface. Unfortunately, none of the other crew members survived. But for one man, the tragedy had ended with a miracle.

A

3 Read the article again. What do these numbers refer to?

0 7   *The number of weeks the miners were trapped underground.*

1	13	3	29	5	33
2	17	4	30	6	60

4 **SPEAKING** Work in pairs. Discuss these questions.

1 What do you think these people did while they were waiting to be rescued?

2 These people had accidents at work. Do you think people should be rescued when they are doing dangerous things for pleasure, for example, climbing mountains? Why (not)?

5 VOCABULARY There are seven highlighted words or phrases in the article. Match them with these definitions.

1 a space where water doesn't get in
2 the history of accidents at a place
3 gone down in the water
4 a terrible event that often kills many people
5 an amazing event that almost seems impossible
6 an instrument that makes a hole in the ground
7 what's left of a car, ship, plane, etc. after a crash

WRITING
A story about a rescue

1 Read the story. Answer the questions.

1 Why did the boy and his friends walk across open land?
2 How long did the rescue take?
3 Why did he need to go to hospital?
4 How did his mother feel about the rescue?

2 Complete the story with the words.

later | and | after | but | which | where | because

3 The story has four paragraphs. Which of them:

a gives details about how the accident happened? ☐
b gives people's reactions to the accident? ☐
c gives a summary of the whole event? ☐
d describes how the accident was dealt with? ☐

4 Think of a rescue that you know about or invent one. Write a story (200 words). Think about:

- who was involved in the accident and the rescue.
- any special words that you will need to talk about the accident. (Use a dictionary to help you.)
- how to organise the information into paragraphs.
- how to make the story dramatic.

1 In March 2014, 14-year-old Za'Quan Clyburn from North Carolina, USA, was rescued ¹_____ he got trapped in mud.

2 Za'Quan was walking home with some friends. To save time, they walked across some open land ²_____ was being prepared for building. Za'Quan walked down a hill towards a large pool of water. He thought the ground was solid ³_____ that he could walk across it, but it was mud. He sank into it and couldn't get out. The mud went up to his chest and then almost to his chin.

3 One of his friends called 911. Fire fighters arrived and started to work to get Za'Quan out. It took 24 people about half an hour to free him. Za'Quan was extremely cold and in shock, and his legs were very painful ⁴_____ of the pressure of the mud. An ambulance took him to hospital, ⁵_____ he was kept for two days.

4 One of the fire fighters said, 'The outcome could have been much worse, ⁶_____ fortunately he came through it OK.' The boy's mother said ⁷_____ that she was really grateful to the people who had worked so hard and risked their lives to save her son.

OBJECTIVES

FUNCTIONS: expressing regret; talking about fears

GRAMMAR: phrasal verbs; *I wish / If only* + past perfect

VOCABULARY: phrasal verbs (2); nervousness and fear

READING

1 **SPEAKING** Look at the photos. Which of these first experiences do *you* remember? Tell your partner. What other things can you remember doing for the first time?

> *I remember my first day at school. I was six and I cried.*

> *I think I can remember the first time I ...*

2 Read the article quickly. Circle the correct word.

In this study, most of the children reported that their earliest memories were *happy / unhappy*.

3 ◀))2.30 Read the article again and listen. Answer the questions.

1 Why did Tom cry?

2 Why did Alice cry?

3 According to this research, is it true that children don't form many memories before their fourth or fifth birthdays?

4 What two things did the researchers ask the children in the first interview?

5 How much time passed between the first and second interviews?

6 What was different in the second interview with the children aged four to seven?

7 How did the children aged ten to 13 reply to the question in the second interview?

8 What question about childhood memories are the researchers trying to answer now?

▮ TRAIN TO THiNK ▮

Logical conclusions

Pay attention to conclusions in a text. Look at the ideas and arguments carefully. Do they lead logically to the conclusion?

4 Here is a conclusion from the article. Which two ideas in the text lead to it? Is it a logical conclusion?

This seems to suggest that our memories change in the early years, but that at around the age of ten, they crystallise.

5 Look at the underlined conclusions. Which aren't logical? Why?

1 Some Bradley Cooper films are brilliant. He's in *Limitless*. It must be a good film.

2 The chef of the restaurant around the corner is famous for his steak. Jane often eats there. Therefore, Jane often eats steak.

3 Apples are very healthy fruit. I often eat apples. I have a healthy diet.

4 Tina has fair skin and burns very easily. She's going to Brazil for a beach holiday. She needs to protect her skin from the sun.

The first thing you remember

'I remember, when I was about three, my mother looking at me in my buggy and smiling at me.'
Jan, 13

'My first memory is my second birthday. There was a cake with two candles. I couldn't ¹<u>blow</u> the candles <u>out</u>, so my dad did it for me.'
Mike, 15

'I remember I was eating an ice cream when a dog came and took it out of my hand. I cried. I was two, I think.'
Tom, 10

'I was maybe four. We were driving to our grandma's and our car ²<u>broke down</u>. We couldn't get out of the car and I cried. A mechanic came to ³<u>sort</u> it <u>out</u>.'
Alice, 12

Most adults remember little about things that happened in their very early childhood. As a result, some people think that we aren't really able to form memories before our fourth or fifth birthdays. But scientists ⁴<u>carrying out</u> research into early memories have suggested that this is untrue. They claim that we do form memories at a very young age. However, what we remember about our very early lives seems to change as we get older.

Researchers in Newfoundland, Canada, worked with 140 children aged between four and 13. First, they asked their participants to describe their earliest memory. Then they asked them roughly how old they'd been when the event occurred. Next, they asked the children's parents to confirm that the event actually happened. All the answers were written down. The researchers waited for two years before they went back to the children and asked them again, 'What's your earliest memory?'

Nearly all the children who were aged between four and seven in the first interview said something very different in the second interview. And when the researchers reminded them of what they'd said the first time, many of the children said: 'No, that never happened to me.' On the other hand, many of the children who were between ten and 13 at the first interview described exactly the same memory in the second interview. This seems to suggest that our memories change in the early years, but that at around the age of ten, they crystallise – the things that we remember get fixed.

The researchers are now ⁵<u>looking into</u> the question of why children remember certain events and not others. We sometimes think that most first or early memories are about very stressful things that happened to us as children, because bad things ⁶<u>stand out</u> in our minds. But in this study, stressful events were only a small percentage of what the children said they remembered. More often, children's early memories were happy ones. The researchers are trying to ⁷<u>work out</u> why this is the case. We can surely ⁸<u>look forward to</u> more fascinating discoveries about memories in the near future.

SPEAKING

Work in pairs. Discuss these questions.

1 What's your first memory? Is it of a nice moment or a stressful event?

2 Is carrying out research on memory important and useful? Why (not)? Who might use this information and how?

VOCABULARY
Phrasal verbs (2)

1 Find the phrasal verbs in the article on page 111. Match them with the definitions.

blow out | break down | sort out
carry out | look into | stand out
work out | look forward to

1 be easy to notice
2 be happy or excited about (a future event)
3 do, complete
4 investigate, examine the facts about (a situation)
5 fix (a problem)
6 use air to stop (something) burning
7 stop working
8 understand, find the answer to

2 Complete the sentences with the correct forms of the phrasal verbs from Exercise 1.

0 The wind _blew_ the candles _out_ on my birthday cake.
1 The concert is tomorrow. I'm really _____ it!
2 Mum was driving to work when her car _____ .
3 There was a bank robbery last Saturday. The police are _____ it.
4 She's our best player. She really _____ in the team.
5 This question is really difficult. I can't _____ the answer.
6 The doctors are _____ tests to find out what's wrong with him.
7 My best friend and I have a problem, but I'm sure we can _____ it _____!

Workbook page 110

GRAMMAR
Phrasal verbs

1 Look at these sentences from the article on page 111. In which ones does the object go between the two parts of the phrasal verb? Then complete the rule with the words.

1 I couldn't blow the candles out.
2 The researchers are now looking into the question of …
3 A mechanic came to sort it out.

between (x2) | separated (x2) | together

> **RULE:** With some phrasal verbs, the two parts can't be [1]_____ . They have to be [2]_____ .
>
> *They're looking into it.*
> NOT ~~They're looking it into.~~
> Other phrasal verbs can be [3]_____ .
> We can put an object [4]_____ the two parts or after the second part.
> *He sorted the problem out.*
> OR *He sorted out the problem.*
>
> When we use a pronoun (*him, it,* etc.) with a phrasal verb that can be separated, it must go [5]_____ the two parts of the verb.
> *He sorted it out.*
> NOT ~~He sorted out it.~~
>
> How do you know if a phrasal verb can be separated? Use a dictionary to look it up!
>
> **look** sth **up** → it **can** be separated
> **look into** sth → it **can't** be separated

2 Put the words in order to make sentences. When there are two possible orders, write both.

0 answer / the / can't / work / I / out
I can't work out the answer.
I can't work the answer out.
1 into / They / the / robbery / are / looking
2 look / We / them / after / have to
3 candles / blew / the / She / out
4 sort / need to / I / problem / the / out

3 **SPEAKING** Complete the questions with the correct forms of the phrasal verbs. Then discuss them in small groups.

look forward to | look after | hang out
give up | sort out | break down

1 What would you do if your bus _____ ten kilometres from where you were going?
2 What are you _____ next weekend?
3 Where do you like to _____ with your friends?
4 What problems do you need to _____?
5 Do you enjoy _____ animals or small children?
6 Do you have any habits you should _____?

Workbook page 108

LISTENING

1 SPEAKING Work in pairs. In what order do you think these Internet innovations happened?

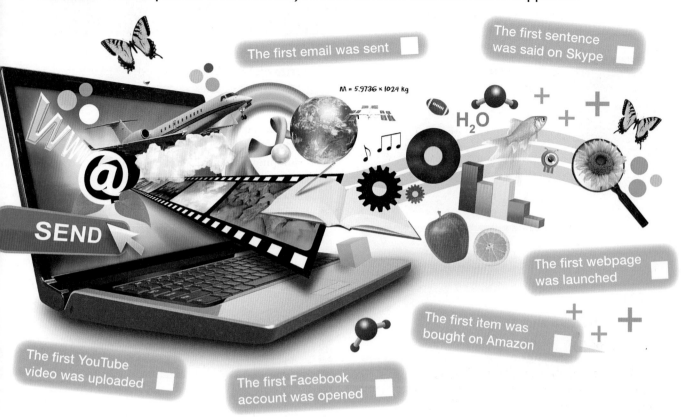

The first email was sent ☐

The first sentence was said on Skype ☐

The first webpage was launched ☐

The first item was bought on Amazon ☐

The first YouTube video was uploaded ☐

The first Facebook account was opened ☐

2 🔊 2.31 Listen to Sally's class presentation about the history of the Internet. Check your answers.

3 🔊 2.31 Listen again. Complete the notes.

> **1 The first website**
> When? _____
> About _____
>
> **2 The first email**
> When? _____
> Sent to? _____
>
> **3 The first Facebook account**
> Number? _____
> Who? _____
>
> **4 The first YouTube video**
> What? _____
> Number of hits? _____
>
> **5 The first item bought on Amazon**
> What? _____
> When? _____
>
> **6 The first sentence spoken on Skype**
> What? _____
> Language _____

4 SPEAKING Work in pairs. Discuss these questions.

1 What other things do we use the Internet to do?
2 What question would you ask Sally?
3 At the end of her presentation, Sally says, 'Who knows where it's going next?' What do you think will be the next big Internet innovations?

▊ THiNK VALUES ▊

Breaking new ground

1 Match the people 1–5 with their achievements a–e.

1 Neil Armstrong ☐
2 Nelson Mandela ☐
3 Yuri Gagarin ☐
4 Kathryn Bigelow ☐
5 Marie Curie ☐

a was the first female director to win an Oscar.
b was the first man on the moon.
c was the first woman to win a Nobel Prize.
d was the first man to travel in space.
e was the first black president of South Africa.

2 SPEAKING Work in small groups. Discuss these questions.

1 Is it important to be the first person to do something? Why (not)?
2 What's more important: coming first (for example, in a competition) or just taking part?

READING

1 **Match 1–4 with the photos.**

1 a jalapeño pepper   3 public speaking
2 bungee jumping   4 a waterslide

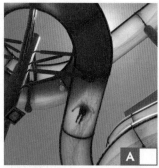 A
 B
 C
 D

2 **SPEAKING** Have you ever done these things? Would you like to? Discuss in small groups.

3 Read the stories and match the writers' names with the photos.

4 Read the stories again. Mark the sentences T (true) or F (false).

1 In the end, Paul jumped.
2 His friend took a photograph of him.
3 Hanif was nervous just before he started speaking.
4 He thinks he spoke well for two minutes.
5 Roseli stayed at the top of the waterslide.
6 She felt OK fifteen minutes later.
7 Ingrid's friend told her what to expect.
8 She didn't feel the full effects of the pepper immediately.

5 Whose story do you think is different from the other three? Why?

6 **SPEAKING** Work in pairs or small groups. What have you only done once? Why?

Pronunciation

Different pronunciations of *ea*
Go to page 121.

MY FIRST (AND LAST) TIME

Is there anything you've only ever done once? Write and tell us about it!

About four years ago, I was on holiday and one day, one of my friends said, 'Hey, there's a bungee jumping place near here! Let's go!' Well, I'd never done anything like that before, but I went anyway. I wish I hadn't gone! I was terrified. I stood there with the rope round my ankle and I was really sweating. In the end, I just panicked and said, 'I can't do this', so they took the rope off. My friend laughed and said, 'If only I'd taken a photo! That was so funny!' I felt really stupid.

Paul, USA

When my older brother got married, he asked me if I'd make a speech at the wedding. I'd never done that before, but I said, 'Sure, OK.' Before the wedding, I thought of a few nice things to say and a couple of jokes. Easy! But on the day, just before I had to speak, I started to get nervous. I was biting my nails and everything. When I stood up, my mouth went dry and I started to tremble – I couldn't believe it! I stumbled through about two minutes of something and sat down again. Two years later, I did a course on public speaking. If only I'd thought of doing that before the wedding!

Hanif, UK

Last year, I went to a beach park. There was a waterslide there which was an incredible 41 metres high. It might sound like fun, but it was one of the most terrifying moments of my life. When I started to fall, I thought, 'I wish I'd stayed up there!' I was petrified the whole time. I still don't know how I did it, and I'm usually OK on rides. I was shaking for about fifteen minutes afterwards, but then I was all right. I'll never do that again, believe me.

Roseli, Brazil

About a year or so ago, we all went to a Mexican restaurant. It was my first time, so I didn't know anything about Mexican food at all. One of my friends told me about jalapeño peppers, and he persuaded me to try one. To be fair, he told me that they were really powerful, and I was a bit anxious when I bit it. At first, it seemed OK, but then it exploded in my mouth! Wow! I started to breathe hard and I had to drink about a hundred glasses of water! That's something I won't do again.

Ingrid, Sweden

GRAMMAR
I wish / If only + past perfect

1 Complete the sentences from the stories on page 114. Use the correct form of the verbs. Then complete the rule.

go | stay | take | know

1 I wish _____ up there!
2 I wish _____ (bungee jumping)!
3 If only _____ a photo!
4 If only _____ of doing that before the wedding!

> **RULE:** To express regret about the past, we can use *I wish* or *If* ¹_____ + the ²_____ tense.

2 Write sentences with *I wish …* or *If only …* .

0 I didn't eat breakfast. Now I'm hungry.
   I wish I'd eaten breakfast.
1 I didn't go to bed early. Now I'm tired.
2 I didn't ask her for her phone number.
3 Only 12 per cent?! I didn't study last weekend.
4 Mum's so angry – Dad forgot her birthday!
5 My friends missed the end of the film. They fell asleep!

3 Think of three things you've done recently that you now regret. Write sentences with *I wish …* and *If only …* .

school | friends | money
family | holidays | shopping

Workbook page 109

FUNCTIONS
Expressing regret

1 Put the lines in order to make a conversation.

☐	OLIVER	I'm sorry to hear that.
☐	OLIVER	What's the matter, Amelia?
☐	OLIVER	Maybe you should lie down for a few minutes.
☐	AMELIA	It was that third piece of cake. I wish I hadn't eaten it.
☐	AMELIA	That isn't a bad idea. I think I will.
☐	AMELIA	I've eaten too much. I'm feeling ill.

2 Work in small groups. Discuss your regrets from Exercise 3 above. Make suggestions using expressions from the conversation in Exercise 1.

> I wish I'd bought a present for my brother's birthday.

> Well, buy one now – it isn't too late!

VOCABULARY
Nervousness and fear

1 Look at the words and phrases in bold in sentences 1–4. Match them with the pictures.

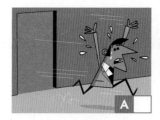

1 I was so **terrified** that I started **biting my nails**.
2 I was really **sweating**. In the end, I just **panicked** and ran out of the room.
3 When I saw the crowd in front of me, my **mouth went dry** and I started to **breathe hard**.
4 I started to **tremble**. In fact, I was **shaking** for about fifteen minutes.

2 SPEAKING Work in pairs. What fears do the photos represent? What other things are some people afraid of?

3 Write sentences about your fears or those of people you know. Use words and phrases from Exercise 1. Then compare with a partner.

My uncle is afraid of heights. He starts to sweat, even if it's just in a film!

Workbook page 110

Fiction

1 ◀》2.34 **Look at the book cover and the title. Read and listen to the introduction. What kind of story is it?**

Bullring Kid and Country Cowboy
by Louise Clover

'Isn't this exciting, Fizza?' said her mum, coming out of the cottage door. 'You can just smell the peace, can't you?' Fizza pretended to yawn. She already knew that this holiday was going to be the most boring one ever.

Fizza McIntyre, a city girl from the huge city of Birmingham, meets her cousin Fletcher McIntyre, a country boy from the tiny island of Sark. An unlikely friendship begins … which leads to an incredible adventure.

2 ◀》2.35 **Read and listen to the rest of the extract. Check your answer.**

Fizza was standing in the middle of a field. Cloudy was on one side of her and Golden was on the other.

'Right,' said Fletcher. 'First! You have to get on – like this!'

And with a simple little jump, he climbed onto Golden.

'Now, you try.'

Nervously, Fizza held onto Cloudy's leather straps and kicked her leg high in the air – unfortunately, at that moment, Cloudy moved and Fizza fell to the ground. Fletcher laughed and laughed. It looked like he was going to fall off his horse.

'No, no, no! You're not fighting with her!' he laughed as, with tears in his eyes, he got off Golden.

'Here, let me help you,' he said, putting out his hand to help her get up.

Fizza was a bit cross at being laughed at and refused to take it at first.

'Oh come on!' he said. 'Hold the saddle, give me your left leg … and now lift your right leg up and over … whoa! Look out!'

Fizza just missed Fletcher's head as she put her leg in the air, but the next thing she knew, she was sitting on top of Cloudy. Fletcher quickly jumped back on Golden.

'OK! Now!' he said. 'Let's go!'

He gave Golden a little kick and they took off across the field very quickly. Fizza's mouth dropped open as she watched them go.

'Is he crazy? I can't do that!' she thought.

However, as Fletcher reached the edge of the field, he turned Golden round and came back to her.

'Why didn't you follow me?' he said, laughing.

Fizza shook her head at him. This guy was crazy … but he was OK.

'I'm not like you! I can't ride like a cowboy!' she said.

'I can't believe you've never ridden before. So what do you do in Birmingham?'

'I spend my time on my computer, I practise judo and I go to the shops at the Bullring sometimes.'

'The Bullring?'

'It's a shopping centre.'

'Do you like shopping?'

'Not really, but my friend Babs does.'

'Oh, I see,' said Fletcher, who couldn't understand why anyone would want to go shopping unless it was for horse food.

'Every cowboy needs a name,' he said, 'and so I'm going to call you … the Bullring Kid!'

For the next two hours Fletcher McIntyre patiently taught Fizza McIntyre how to ride a horse. They started by walking the horses slowly and, little by little, he got Fizza to go a little faster. Once, when Cloudy went a bit too fast, Fizza became very frightened.

'I can't stop!' she cried out. 'I can't stop!'

Quickly, Fletcher chased after her, took Cloudy's straps and stopped her. He could see that she was crying.

'It's OK, it's OK, Fizza,' he said kindly. 'You're doing really well – I won't let you get hurt. I promise.'

And Fletcher kept his promise. Very gently and very patiently, he taught Fizza how to ride.

3 Read the extract again. Answer the questions.

1 What are the names of the two horses? Who rides each horse?

2 Why does Fletcher have 'tears in his eyes'?

3 Why doesn't Fizza want to take Fletcher's hand?

4 What is Fizza's reason for going shopping in Birmingham?

5 What nickname does Fletcher give her? Why?

6 How do we know that Fizza didn't get hurt?

4 **SPEAKING** Work in pairs. Discuss these questions.

1 Do you think that Fletcher treats Fizza badly? Why (not)?

2 Fletcher gives Fizza a nickname. Would you be happy if someone did that to you? Why (not)?

3 What do you think will happen next?

WRITING
A story about a bad decision

1 Read the story. What was Pauline's bad decision, according to the writer?

2 Find sentences in the story with these meanings. How are the <u>underlined</u> phrases expressed in the story?

1 <u>Pauline regretted the fact that she'd gone</u> to university.

2 <u>It's a pity that you didn't tell</u> us.

3 <u>I think it's a pity that she didn't tell</u> her parents.

4 <u>It isn't good that Pauline didn't make</u> her own decision.

3 The story has four paragraphs. Which of them:

a is about a decision that the person made?

b gives background information about the person?

c gives the writer's thoughts about the whole situation?

d explains the effects of the decision?

4 Think of a (true or invented) story about a bad decision. Write your story (200 words). Think about:

• who the person is / was.

• the situation the person was in which meant that he/she had to make a decision.

• the decision that the person made.

• what happened after making the decision.

• what you or the person felt about it all afterwards.

LEARNING FROM EXPERIENCE?

We asked readers to tell us stories about bad decisions they or people they know have made. Here's this week's story.

1 A friend of mine has a sister, Pauline, who's six years older than him. She was always good at school, but all she really wanted to do was to help her parents in their small shop, and then perhaps take it over when they were too old to run it.

2 Pauline's parents, however, really wanted her to go to university, so she spent three years at school working incredibly hard, studying for an exam for a famous university in another city. She passed, and a few months later she left home to start studying there.

3 From the first moment, Pauline wished she hadn't gone to university. She hated it. She'd been a clever student at school, but the university work was much harder. She didn't make many friends either, so she was lonely and homesick. After six months, she asked her parents to let her leave and come home. They were very surprised when she said that she'd never wanted to go to university. 'If only you'd told us!' they said. 'But I didn't want to disappoint you,' was her answer.

4 Now Pauline is working in the shop and she's very happy. I wish she'd told her parents that university wasn't what she wanted – then she wouldn't have wasted six months of her life. Pauline should have made her own decision.

READING AND USE OF ENGLISH
Part 6: Gapped text

Workbook page 107

You are going to read about someone travelling abroad for the first time.
Six sentences have been removed from the text. Choose from the sentences (A–G) the one that fits each gap (1–6). There is one extra sentence that you do not need to use.

My first flight

I've never really enjoyed travelling very much. The idea of leaving the comfort of my own bed to sleep somewhere else has never appealed to me. And when you add in things like the food and not being understood, the thought of leaving my home town fills me with terror. I did go away on a school trip once, when I was eight, for two nights. My mother tells me I quite enjoyed the experience. (**1**) _____ There must be a reason why I can't remember anything positive about it.

So for 28 years I'd managed to lead a life that kept me happily at home. A few nights in hotels for work had been the worst I'd had to go through. Then, one day, my boss called me in. He shook my hand. He was smiling from one ear to the other. (**2**) _____
'Paul!' he announced. 'You've been promoted.'
I should have been happy, I suppose, but something in the back of my mind was telling me this wasn't 100 per cent good news. (**3**) _____
'Of course, you'll need extra training. I've booked you on a course at head office in Linz. Your flight's on Monday.'

I started to feel dizzy. I had to hold on to the table to stop myself from falling. My boss patted me on the back.
'Great news, eh?' he smiled. Then he left the room.

So that was it. Just when my professional life had got better, the rest of my life was over. No one had ever survived an aeroplane flight, had they?

(**4**) _____ I wasn't so sure. I spent the weekend making my final farewells as Monday morning got closer.

(**5**) _____ Before I knew it, my taxi had left me at the airport. Somehow I made my way to the check-in desk. I lifted my suitcase onto the conveyor belt and walked through airport security to the lounge. I have no idea how I knew what to do. I guess that because I'd seen it so many times in films, it was programmed into my mind.

The flight was only two hours. (**6**) _____ I tried to read a book, but I couldn't. I tried listening to my MP3 player – I'd chosen some relaxing music especially – but it sounded like it was being played by an orchestra of three-year-olds. Every sound the plane made sent my imagination spinning out of control. Was that the sound of the wing falling off? Was that a bird being sucked through an engine? Was that the noise of wheels hitting the runway? Yes, it was. We had landed.

Somehow we'd arrived. I wanted to grab my fellow travellers and celebrate the fact that we were still alive, but they were all busy getting their luggage from the overhead lockers. So I celebrated on my own. But then I remembered: unless I wanted to spend the rest of my life in Austria, I still had to fly back!

A What wasn't right about this?
B My family and friends tried to assure me that of course they had.
C I thought that it was never going to end.
D And then the day I had been dreading arrived.
E Would I ever see my wife again?
F It wasn't long before I found out why.
G That certainly isn't what my memory tells me.

VOCABULARY

1   Complete the sentences with the words / phrases in the list. There are four extra words / phrases.

broke down | afraid | illogical | work out | looking forward to | panicked | informal
hang out | looking into | sort out | mouth went dry | irresponsible | impatient | look up

1   I don't know what 'resolution' means. I'm going to _____ it _____ in the dictionary.
2   I can't come climbing with you. No way! I'm _____ of heights.
3   My friends and I usually _____ in the park when the weather's good.
4   The show didn't go very well – I _____ when I walked on stage, and then I forgot what I wanted to say.
5   It was snowing heavily when the car _____!
6   Don't be so _____ . It'll be your turn soon.
7   I'm _____ going on holiday next week.
8   I can't _____ the answer to this question. Can you help me?
9   It was very _____ of you to go swimming in the sea during the storm.
10   The police are _____ the mugging and they want to speak to this man.

/10

GRAMMAR

2   Complete the sentences with the words / phrases in the list. There are two extra words / phrases.

I wish | If | only | such | feel like | afford | so | in order to

1   It was _____ a loud noise that everybody in the street heard it.
2   He jumped into the lake _____ rescue the boy.
3   I don't _____ going swimming. It's too cold.
4   He can't _____ to buy that computer game. He owes Tom some money.
5   Everyone laughs at my hair. If _____ I hadn't dyed it green!
6   _____ you'd waited for me. Then this wouldn't have happened.

3   Find and correct the mistake in each sentence.

1   It's a big problem now. We need to sort out it.
2   My friends and I really hated to bungee jumping last weekend.
3   I'm such hungry! I'll have to eat something now.
4   They're going to cover the hole so to prevent future accidents.
5   It was so a bad car crash that nobody survived.
6   After the accident, my dad promised wearing a seat belt in future.

/12

FUNCTIONAL LANGUAGE

4   Circle the correct words.

1   A   The police want to increase the fine to £1,000 *so as / so* to stop people driving so fast.
    B   I think that's *so / such* a good idea.
2   A   What's the *shame / matter*, Erika?
    B   I'm feeling a bit ill. I wish I *hadn't / haven't* eaten all that cake.
3   A   Let's have a book sale *in / on* order to make some money for the school.
    B   That's not a bad *thought / idea*.

/8

4   A   His headache was *so / such* bad that he couldn't concentrate on the exam and failed.
    B   I'm sorry to hear *this / that*.

MY SCORE	/30
22 – 30	
10 – 21	
0 – 9	

PRONUNCIATION

UNIT 1
Linking words with *up*

1 🔊 1.11 **Read and listen to the dialogue.**

STEVE   What's **up**, Jenny?
JENNY   I'm tired! I'**m up** late every night studying.
STEVE   You need your sleep! Can't you ge**t up** later?
JENNY   Not really. I've take**n up** the flute this year. I practise in the mornings.
STEVE   Well, it'**s up** to you, but I'd give tha**t up**!
JENNY   Hmmm … I wish I hadn't signe**d up** for the school orchestra now!

2 **What happens to the words in blue?** (Circle) **the correct word to complete the rule:**

A word ending in a *consonant* / *vowel* sound links with the following word when it begins with a *consonant* / *vowel* sound.

3 🔊 1.12 **Listen, repeat and practise.**

UNIT 2
Initial consonant clusters with /s/

1 🔊 1.14 **Read and listen to the tongue twisters.**

Strong winds **sp**read the **sp**arks through the **st**reets.
Stella's got **st**raight hair and **st**ripes on her **sk**irt.
Stewart **sp**rayed his phone with a **sp**ecial **scr**een cleaner.

2 **Say the words in blue.**

3 🔊 1.15 **Listen, repeat and practise.**

UNIT 3
Strong and weak forms: /ɒv/ and /əv/

1 🔊 1.21 **Read and listen to the dialogue.**

JULIA   What do you always buy the same brand **of**?
JACK   I always buy the same brand **of** trainers. They're called Ace. I bought a pair **of** green ones last week.
JULIA   Ace? What are they made **of**?
JACK   They're made **of** fabric and rubber. They put a lot **of** effort into the design and quality **of** them.
JULIA   And into the marketing **of** them, too!

2 🔊 1.21 **Listen again and** underline **each of which is stressed and** (circle) **each of which is unstressed.**

3 🔊 1.22 **Listen, repeat and practise.**

UNIT 4
Consonant–vowel word linking

1 🔊 1.28 **Read and listen to the dialogue.**

LISA   I was only joking, but I wish I hadn't said it. I think she hates me.
HENRY   Well, it was unkind of you to say you didn't like her new haircut.
LISA   I know! I can't believe I said that she looked like a boy! It just came out. What should I do?
HENRY   First, I'd apologise. Then I'd admit that I prefer it long. Actually, I think she looks amazing!

2 🔊 1.28 Underline **examples of linking in the dialogue. Then listen and check.**

3 🔊 1.29 **Listen, repeat and practise.**

UNIT 5
The schwa /ə/ in word endings

1 🔊 1.35 **Read and listen to the tongue twisters.**

Ireland's a nation with famous traditions.
My neighbour's a brilliant classical musician.
The monster's a villain who frightens the children.

2 🔊 1.35 **Listen again and focus on the syllables in blue. Are they stressed or unstressed? They all have the same short vowel sound. What is it?**

3 🔊 1.36 **Listen, repeat and practise.**

UNIT 6
The /ʒ/ phoneme

1 🔊 1.39 **Read and listen to the interview.**

HELEN   Welcome to *Film Night Television*. Our guest is Tom Potts, who stars in an unusual thriller called *Asian Treasure*. Why did you decide to take on this role?
TOM   It was a difficult decision, Helen. I play the part of an amazing illusionist.
HELEN   There are so many collisions and explosions in the film that I thought you would never find that treasure.
TOM   It's true! Occasionally I was frightened for my own life!

2 🔊 1.39 **How is each 's' in blue pronounced?**

3 🔊 1.40 **Listen, repeat and practise.**

UNIT 7

Intonation – inviting, accepting and refusing invitations

1 🔊 2.06 **Read and listen to the dialogue.**

MAX	Hi, Gina! I'm organising a hiking trip. Why don't you come along?
GINA	Thank you, Max. I'd love to. When are you going?
MAX	Next Saturday. We're going to climb Mount Sunrise. How about bringing some friends?
GINA	That's a great idea! Oh … I'm already going out on Saturday. What a shame. I'm sorry, Max.

2 🔊 2.06 Underline the two invitations and the sentences where Gina accepts and refuses the invitation. What happens to Max and Gina's voice in each case? Listen again and check.

3 🔊 2.07 Listen, repeat and practise.

UNIT 8

Intonation – expressing surprise

1 🔊 2.12 **Read and listen to the dialogue.**

JACKSON	You're not going to believe this.
MARYANNE	Tell me.
JACKSON	School's closed for the rest of the term!
MARYANNE	What?
JACKSON	The police said there was an urgent situation but didn't give any details.
MARYANNE	That's awful!
JACKSON	And the principal said she's extremely sorry but there's nothing she can do!
MARYANNE	Really?

2 🔊 2.12 Listen again and underline all of the words which are stressed.

3 🔊 2.13 Listen, repeat and practise.

UNIT 9

Moving word stress

1 🔊 2.15 **Read and listen to the dialogues.**

1 A Do you know the **mystery** of Amelia Earhart?
  B Yes – her disappearance is very **mysterious**!

2 A Wow! That's a great **photograph**.
  B Thanks! I'm really into **photography**.

3 A If we go to this summer camp, we can do the course on **navigation**.
  B But I already know how to **navigate**.

2 Underline the stressed syllables in the words in blue. Say the two words in blue in each dialogue.

3 🔊 2.16 Listen, repeat and practise.

UNIT 10

Short and long vowel sounds: /ɪ/ – /iː/ and /ɒ/ – /əʊ/

1 🔊 2.21 **Read and listen to the dialogues.**

MRS GREEN	We all need good self esteem. But what does it mean? Tim?
TIM	It's a lot of things, Mrs Green. But it's really important to feel happy to be as we are.
MR ROSS	So, do you copy your favourite pop stars? Do you wear the same clothes, Rose?
ROSE	Mr Ross! I follow pop stars – but I don't wear the same clothes! I'm not a clone.

2 Say the words with the *short* /ɪ/ and the *long* /iː/ sounds. How does your mouth change shape? Say the words with the *short* /ɒ/ and the *long* /əʊ/ sounds. How does your mouth change shape now?

3 🔊 2.22 Listen, repeat and practise.

UNIT 11

Strong and weak forms: /tuː/ and /tə/

1 🔊 2.26 **Read and listen to the dialogue.**

STEVE	Hi, Jane! It's good to see you. What have you been up to?
JANE	I've been travelling. I've been to so many places, I couldn't name them all!
STEVE	Wow, that's exciting. Did you go to Germany?
JANE	Well … that's one place I didn't get to. I went to France and Spain, though.

2 Say the words in blue with the weak form of *to*. Now say the words in red in the strong form.

3 🔊 2.27 Listen, repeat and practise.

UNIT 12

Different pronunciations of *ea*

1 🔊 2.32 **Read and listen to the dialogue.**

TEACHER	Has everyone read the article about healthy living?
JEAN	I have, sir. From the research I learned that we have to look after ourselves from an early age.
TEACHER	Yes, it would appear that every year counts. Are there any more ideas?
HEATHER	Eating and sleeping well is really important, Mr Heath.
TEACHER	Great answer. Now let's take a break!

2 How many different pronunciations of the *ea* spelling are there? Say the highlighted words.

3 🔊 2.33 Listen, repeat and practise.

GET IT RIGHT!

UNIT 1

Present simple vs. present continuous

It's common to confuse the present simple and present continuous.

We use the present simple to describe facts, routine activities and opinions.

✓ I *usually go* there on foot.
✗ I'm usually going there on foot.

We use the present continuous to describe events that are happening now or around now.

✓ I'm *sending* you a photo of my new bike.
✗ I send you a photo of my new bike.

Find the error in each of these sentences. Rewrite the sentences correctly.

0   I know how hard you try to get on the team.
    I know how hard you are trying to get on the team.

1   I think I am the person you look for.
    _____
    _____

2   I'm playing tennis on Tuesdays.
    _____
    _____

3   At the moment I write a letter to a friend.
    _____
    _____

4   I like what you wear today.
    _____
    _____

5   I know what you mean and are appreciating your help.
    _____
    _____

6   We are playing football during most school breaks.
    _____
    _____

UNIT 2

Present perfect vs. past simple

Students often confuse the present perfect and past simple tenses.

We use the past simple when we include a past time expression to say when in the past an event took place.

✓ Yesterday I *ate* rice.
✗ Yesterday I have eaten rice.

We use the present perfect to talk about past events when we don't say exactly when they took place and with expressions such as *yet*, *before*, *ever* and *never*.

✓ I've never **been** to London before.
✗ I didn't go to London before.

Make sentences using the prompts below.

0   we / see / the advertisement at the bus stop / yesterday
    We saw the advertisement at the bus stop yesterday.

1   I / not see / the new Hobbit film / yet
    _____
    _____

2   you / ever / go / to Spain?
    _____
    _____

3   John / take / his exam / last week
    _____
    _____

4   Nina / get / here / a few minutes ago
    _____
    _____

5   they / not eat / at this restaurant / before
    _____
    _____

6   I / not eat / breakfast / so I'm really hungry and it's two hours till lunchtime!
    _____
    _____

Past continuous vs. past simple

> **Learners sometimes confuse the past continuous with the past simple.**
>
> ✓ *I was happy when I **came** first in the race.*
> ✗ *I was happy when I ~~was coming~~ first in the race.*

Which of these sentences are correct and which are incorrect? Rewrite the incorrect ones.

0   Last time I was visiting the library, I couldn't find the book I was looking for.

Last time I visited the library, I couldn't find the book I was looking for.

1   When she arrived, I cooked dinner so I was a bit distracted.

2   After that, I watched TV for about an hour.

3   As usual, we were arriving at about 6 pm, then we had dinner.

4   My teacher came to see how our project went.

5   I'll never forget the time I was spending in Nepal.

6   The police saw the men and asked them what they did there.

UNIT 3
have to vs. had to

> **Learners sometimes confuse *have to* and *had to*.**
>
> **We use *have to* to talk about an obligation in the present, and *had to* to talk about an obligation in the past.**
>
> ✓ *Shopping is stressful, especially if you **have to** find a particular item of clothing.*
> ✗ *Shopping is stressful, especially if you ~~had to~~ find a particular item of clothing.*

Which of these sentences are correct and which are incorrect? Rewrite the incorrect ones.

0   The trains were fully booked so we have to forget about that trip.

The trains were fully booked so we had to forget about that trip.

1   I'm sorry I can't attend class tomorrow because I had to go to the doctor.

2   My dad was going to work for another company so we have to move house.

3   If you want a drink after swimming, you have to go somewhere else.

4   If I have to choose between going to a small school or a large one, I would choose a large one.

5   Do we have to bring any money for the trip next week?

6   Yesterday we had to write an essay about Barack Obama.

don't have to vs. mustn't

> **Learners sometimes make errors with *don't have to* and *mustn't*.**
>
> **Although *have to* and *must* both mean something is necessary, *don't have to* means that something is <u>not necessary</u>, whereas *mustn't* means that something is <u>prohibited</u>.**
>
> ✓ *I **don't have to** work tonight, as I've already finished everything.*
> ✗ *I ~~mustn't~~ work tonight, as I've already finished everything.*
> ✓ *I **mustn't** fail my exam, or I'll have to retake it.*

Write the sentences with *mustn't* or *don't have to*.

0   You / stay out late or you'll be really tired tomorrow.

You mustn't stay out late or you'll be really tired tomorrow.

1   You / finish your essay now. Mr Jenkins said that we can hand it in next Friday.

2   You / bring anything to the party – just bring yourself!

3   You / eat food in class – it's against the rules.

4   You / talk during exams.

5   You / revise every unit. The exam only includes Units 1 to 3.

6   You / use your phone in class. It'll be confiscated.

UNIT 4
if vs. when

> Learners often confuse *if* with *when*.
>
> **We use *if* to indicate possible actions or events.**
>
> ✓ *It'll be best for us **if** everyone goes by bicycle. Car parking facilities are limited.*
> ✗ *It'll be best for us ~~when~~ everyone goes by bicycle. Car parking facilities are limited.*
>
> **We use *when* to indicate events which have happened in the past or are going to happen in the future.**
>
> ✓ *I can pass on your message. I'll tell him **when** I see him tomorrow.*
> ✗ *I can pass on your message. I'll tell him ~~if~~ I see him tomorrow.*

Complete these sentences with *if* or *when*.

0   I was very pleased _when_ I read your letter.
1   I had a great time _____ I went to New York.
2   Would it be OK _____ I invited my friend?
3   I'll call you _____ I get home tonight.
4   Do you mind _____ we meet at 5.00 instead of 4.00?
5   _____ you're free on Saturday, come to the cinema with us!
6   He went to Africa _____ he was 21 because of his job.
7   How much would it cost _____ we were a group of ten?

UNIT 5
Relative pronouns

> Learners sometimes confuse *who* and *which*.
>
> **We use *who* to refer to people and *which* to refer to things.**
>
> ✓ *Next week I'm going to visit my Uncle Joe, **who** lives in Manchester.*
> ✗ *Next week I'm going to visit my Uncle Joe, ~~which~~ lives in Manchester.*

Complete the sentences with *who* or *which*.

0   There are several problems _which_ can't wait any longer.
1   My friend Paul, _____ I've known since primary school, is coming.
2   Animals _____ can protect themselves shouldn't be kept in a zoo.
3   My dad works for a company _____ sells dental products.

4   It's a great film but it's really sad. It's about a soldier _____ goes to war.
5   She was the only one _____ talked to me.
6   He's currently working for a charity _____ helps elderly people.

UNIT 6
absolutely vs. very

> A common mistake is using intensifiers like *absolutely* and *very* with the wrong types of adjectives.
>
> **We use *absolutely* to modify non-gradable adjectives or adjectives with a strong or extreme meaning.**
>
> ✓ *It's **absolutely** delicious.*
> ✗ *It's ~~very~~ delicious.*
>
> **We use *very* to modify gradable adjectives.**
>
> ✓ *I was **very** disappointed with it.*
> ✗ *I was ~~absolutely~~ disappointed with it.*

Complete the sentences with *absolutely* or *very*.

0   In my opinion, the countryside is _very_ relaxing.
1   This museum is _____ fascinating.
2   The view from the top was _____ amazing.
3   I thought the documentary was _____ interesting.
4   I was _____ thrilled to get an 'A' on that assignment.
5   This food is _____ tasty.
6   She's a _____ good singer.

UNIT 7
make vs. let

> Learners sometimes confuse *make* and *let* in phrases such as *let me know*.
>
> ✓ *You were on TV and you didn't **let** us know!*
> ✗ *You were on TV and you didn't ~~make~~ us know!*

Complete the sentences with the correct form of *make* or *let*.

0   There are great views which will _make_ you feel very comfortable.
1   _____ me help you with that bag. It looks really heavy.
2   The band came on stage late. They _____ us wait over an hour.
3   That TV documentary about diet and health really _____ me think about doing more exercise.
4   Mum, can you write a note to my teacher to _____ her know why I won't be in class tomorrow?

5   It's so important to _____ people aware of the disease so that we can raise money to help prevent it.

6   It was very kind of you to _____ us stay over, Mrs Johnson. Thanks very much for having us!

UNIT 8
say vs. *tell*

> Learners sometimes confuse *say* and *tell*.
>
> The meaning of *say* and *tell* is exactly the same but we use them differently.
>
> We *tell someone* (*something*) and we *say something* (*to someone*).
>
> ✓ I didn't **say anything to** my brother about it.
> ✗ I didn't ~~tell anything to~~ my brother about it.
>
> We can also use a *that* clause immediately after *tell*, but not after *say*.
>
> ✓ **Tell her that** I'll phone her.
> ✗ ~~Say her that~~ I'll phone her.
>
> There are some collocations we can use with *tell* that don't follow the above rules: we can *tell a lie / the truth / a story*.

Complete each of these sentences with the correct form of *say* or *tell*.

0   Everybody *said* something about himself, and so did I.

1   I have to _____ that this is a great piece of writing. Well done!

2   You're going to have to _____ him that you can't play in Saturday's match. You're injured.

3   _____ us the story of how you met.

4   Did he _____ why he lied?

5   My mum _____ that we were going to move house.

6   I'd like to _____ a big thank you for all your help this year.

7   I knew that he _____ the truth.

UNIT 9
Modals of deduction in the present

> It is a common error to use *can* as a present modal of deduction, where *could* is required. In the negative, however, it is possible to use *can't* as well as *couldn't*.
>
> ✓ I'm not sure why they decided not to buy tickets to see the band, but it **could be** due to lack of money.
> ✗ I'm not sure why they decided not to buy tickets to see the band, but it ~~can be~~ due to lack of money.
> ✓ The reason **can't be** a lack of interest.

Which of these sentences are correct and which are incorrect? Rewrite the incorrect ones.

0   Where's John? He can be at home.
    Where's John? He could be at home.

1   A   Do you have a better idea for how to get there?
    B   Well, I think another route can be better.
    _____

2   A   Does he need help?
    B   He can do. It looks like he might be waving for us to stop.
    _____

3   A   How does that car go so fast?
    B   It can be because it's so light. Just a guess!
    _____

4   A   What do you think is going to happen in the game?
    B   They could still win or maybe it'll be a draw.
    _____

5   A   Is Dad still at work?
    B   The car's outside. He can't be.
    _____

6   A   Who made the complaint?
    B   It could be Nick – he didn't think there was a problem.
    _____

UNIT 10
Future continuous vs. future simple

> Learners often confuse the future continuous with the future simple.
>
> We use the future continuous to talk about events which will be in the process of happening at some time in the future.
>
> ✓ This time next week **I'll be sitting** on the beach in Cádiz.
> ✗ This time next week ~~I'll sit~~ on the beach in Cádiz.

Decide if the sentences can be written in the future continuous. If so, rewrite them using this tense. What's the difference in meaning between the future simple and future continuous form in these cases?

0   When you get to the station, I'll wait for you at the main entrance.
    When you get to the station, I'll be waiting for you at the main entrance.

1   This time next year we'll be at university and we'll live away from home.
    _____

2 I'll have a look in my diary and see if I'm free on the 5th.

3 This time next week I'll do my final exams. Scary!

4 Some people think that tablets will soon replace laptops.

5 I'll play hockey when you arrive at the station tomorrow but Chloe can meet you.

6 I think you'll have a good time when you go to Spain.

UNIT 11
Verbs patterns

> Learners sometimes make errors with verb patterns, using *to* + infinitive when it should be a gerund and vice versa.
> ✓ I **don't mind going** home first.
> ✗ I ~~don't mind to go~~ home first.

Which of these sentences are correct and which are incorrect? Rewrite the incorrect ones.

0 He's always had problems to focus on one task.
He's always had problems focussing on one task.

1 Do you need more time finishing your work?

2 Lately I've been spending a lot of time to watch TV.

3 I need to start working on my essay as soon as possible.

4 It was a very heavy film, but we enjoyed to learn about history.

5 It's best studying new vocabulary regularly.

6 I had real difficulties downloading this app but I got there eventually.

UNIT 12
Phrasal verbs

> Learners sometimes avoid using phrasal verbs, using single, often Latinate, verbs instead. Using phrasal verbs can make you sound more natural and increase the variety of your English.
> ✓✓ Students were **put up** in hotels.
> ✓ Students were **accommodated** in hotels.

Replace the verbs in bold with phrasal verbs from the list.

put up with ┃ put on ┃ put up (x3) ┃ put off

0 Before I went to the beach, I **applied** sun cream.
Before I went to the beach, I put on sun cream.

1 Our family has agreed to **host** a foreign student for a month during the summer.

2 One advantage of taking the train is that you don't have to **tolerate** traffic jams.

3 I don't get to exercise so much anymore and I'm worried about **gaining** weight.

4 Good news! We're going to have to **postpone** today's test until next Friday.

5 Cinema tickets were already expensive and now they've just **increased** the prices again.

6 We **displayed** posters to advertise the event.

STUDENT A

UNIT 1, PAGE 19

Student A

You aren't very happy with your brother or sister. He/She plays loud music that you don't like when you're trying to work. He/She doesn't even keep the door closed. What else upsets you about this? You have decided to talk to him/her about it. Try and use the expressions in Exercise 1.

Excuse me, [name], I need a word ...

UNIT 7, PAGE 73

Student A

1   Invite your partner to do these things with you. Then add one more idea of your own.

- Watch a football match at the local sports ground.
- Meet some of your friends and go to the shopping centre.

2   Accept or refuse your partner's invitations.

STUDENT B

UNIT 1, PAGE 19

Student B

You aren't very happy with your brother or sister. He/She keeps taking your clothes without asking you. He/She makes a real mess when he/she takes them from your wardrobe. What else upsets you about this? You have decided to talk to him/her about it. Try and use the expressions in Exercise 1.

Excuse me, [name], I need a word ...

UNIT 7, PAGE 73

Student B

1 Accept or refuse your partner's invitations.

2 Invite your partner to do these things with you. Then add one more idea of your own.

- Watch a horror DVD at your place.
- Go for a long walk in the mountains.